What Moms and Dads are Saying...

"Amazing book. I'm a single father who at first thought this book was only for mothers, but soon realized it's for everyone! Through my recent divorce and frustrations with single parenting, I have been going CRAZY, and felt as if there was no hope for me *or* my children. I instantly applied the ideas and principles from *Upside-Down Mommy*, and I noticed a huge transformation. I'm looking forward to consistently using *Upside-Down Mommy* as a staple in my mental health diet, and I will pass these timeless principles down to my two beautiful children."

~ Joel Russell Lane ~
Single Father of Two

"There really are no words worthy to describe the journey that this book took me on. I know it's *Upside-Down Mommy*, but the lessons are not just for mothers or even parents. We were all children once and experienced the limiting beliefs, poor examples, and all of the other crap. And this book shows us how to get over it...*really* get over it. It's such a personal story, yet it is actually everyone's story. Thank you for being open, vulnerable, and honest."

~ LaVonne Shields ~
Mom and Founder of
Management Consultants of America

"Creatively written, *Upside-Down Mommy* brilliantly intertwines adult and child experiences, taking the reader on a journey that transcends logic, reaching and captivating the soul. I highly recommend this transformational book as a resource for the educational, judicial, social service, and mental health systems, as well as parents and adult children."

~ Dr. Sandy Ingle, PhD ~
'Mom' to Those with Broken Wings,
Clinical Psychologist and Counselor

"Being a mom to a 'tween' daughter, Amanda's 'Butterfly Approach to Parenting' truly spoke to a need I have felt to change my parenting style. *Upside-Down Mommy* is a book for every mom who wants to heal her own story and understand how to nurture in her children a 'no limits' mindset. Regardless of how old your children are, it's never too late to help them discover the 'Magic Egg' inside!"

~ Marlia Cochran ~
Mommy, Speaker, Author of
Where's My White Picket Fence:
When A Good Girl Doubts God,
and Co-Host of Elevate4Women Radio

"As a pastor and spiritual life coach, I believe that understanding Amanda's 'Magic Egg' and the implementation of her 'Butterfly Approach to Parenting' has the power to start a revolution that will drastically reduce future crime, domestic violence, addiction, and child abuse. I consider this a 'must read' for parents, teachers, and child advocates."

~ Tami Dempsey ~
Mommy, Founder of Pastor Tami Ministries
(including Dreamkeepers4Kids), and
Court Appointed Special Advocate (CASA)
for abused and neglected children

"Symbols are crucial to the spiritual journey of a human, as we are energy in flesh and vibrational frequencies at our core. That is what makes this book so exceptional, with its layers of metamorphosis and self-inquiry, that we can become students as parents in our interactions with our children. At the same time, Amanda takes us on a new path of going ever deeper into consciousness to become the butterflies we already, always were. Read at your own risk. If you are ready to transform, this book is for you."

~ Leta Hamilton ~
Mommy, Channel to the Angels, "Mission Statement for Motherhood" Creator, Author of *The Way of the Toddler*, Radio Show Host and Keynote Speaker

"This book will turn your beliefs about traditional parenting UPSIDE-DOWN in the best possible way. Amanda is a clear voice in supporting all of us in following our own intuition and internal guidance and power, whether 6 years old or 60 years old. She is a mom and woman who truly walks the talk, staying true to her intention both in her personal life and her business."

~ Cheryl Herrick ~
Mommy, Founder of Ponytail Racing
(Transformational Racing Events),
and Author of *I Asked*

"Although Amanda Johnson's book, *Upside-Down Mommy*, is an inspiring journal to her beloved son, it is written with such honesty, insight, and unconditional love that it could be a manual to anyone for living life. The pages illustrate the art of forgiveness, trusting one's inner voice, and recognizing that everyone has value regardless of age or station in life. This book is a guide to be a positive impact on whomever crosses one's path — what an awesome legacy."

~ Peggy Ricks ~
Mommy and Founder of
First Impression

"A jewel of a book! Amanda's transparency and willingness to tell her story, uglies and all, enable an understanding of her concepts, and even a hope of a brighter future if you choose a legacy without limits for your children and yourself."

~ Renée E. Cabourne ~
Step-mom, CFP®, Founder of
Money Savvy Woman™

"Amanda's *Upside-Down Mommy* reminded me of so many people's stories. Her relatable insights and personal stories illustrate the importance of mastering our major life role as both a teacher and a student. She shows us how to live our lives through the eyes of a child, but walk with the confident stride of a wise and experienced adult. I highly recommend this book for any mother who is looking for a dose of courage in order to clean up early childhood deficits that may be playing havoc in loving relationships."

~ Maggie Bain ~
Mommy, Transformational Speaker,
Relationship and Intimacy Coach,
Founder of Rock Solid Love, and
Author of *Love On The Rock:
Take Your Love Life from
'Ho-Hum' to Extraordinary*

"*Upside-Down Mommy* is uplifting and inspires a universal call to action for all parents to shift to empowered parenting; and I believe all people who have children, work with children, or want to have children can gather immense power, strength, and wisdom from Amanda's 'Butterfly Approach to Parenting.' Enjoy the journey to transform your parenting with her as you contribute to changing the world one family at a time."

~ Dr. Pam Denton ~
Rockin' Mommy, Founder of
PKD Wellness, and
Author of *Be Heal Live:*
Shift from Crisis to Clarity

"In this compelling, transformational book, Amanda takes the reader into her own parenting journey of healing her stories of shame and disconnection from herself. Her 'Butterfly Approach to Parenting' guides parents, and anyone working with children, to create a safe space for themselves and the children they care for, to evolve and emerge without the constraints that keep humans limited and unable to live to their fullest potential. This book will leave you desiring more in your life and in your child's life. It's not a 'how-to' book; it's an experience."

~ Jacqueline VanCampen ~
Mommy, Founder and
CEO of Wise Heart Within,
and Author of *Letters to*
My Daughter: A Mother's Journey
of Healing and Transformation

"*Upside-Down Mommy* is a beautifully transparent and powerfully vulnerable book that shines light on the power of the journey to finding and living one's life-purpose, using faith, love, truth, and compassion. As a mom myself, Amanda has empowered me to be aware and listen to the mirrors that appear in my life, especially when they are my kids, and how to impact and empower each other to live with no imits as a family."

~ Jennifer Griner ~
Mom and Founder of the
National Association for Balanced Moms

"I know this book is going to change America and spread across the world because every parent, educator, and anyone who works with kids MUST read it. I laughed and cried through Amanda's engaging stories and powerful lessons, thinking, 'Wow, if every kid (and parent) on the planet could learn to listen to their own inner voice, be aware and relax into the natural processes of growth, create and maintain healthy boundaries, focus on the impact they want to bring to the world, and have a sacred safe place to do it...OMG, can you imagine that new world?' It's an easy and fairly short read, but don't let that fool you. It's packed with amazing tools, and I'm so glad I read it and can apply these tools in my work, and in the family I plan to start with my husband in the next few years."

~ Jenee Dana ~
Future Mommy, Founder of My Focus Book, and Award-winning & #1 Bestselling Author of *Have Fun & Get It Done*

"I couldn't put *Upside-Down Mommy* down until I read the last page. It is truly an insightful and inspiring book. I particularly admired the metaphors used throughout the book to portray the challenges and beauty of life, love, and parenting.

As a parent and an energy healer, I enjoyed reading about the thought-provoking healing journey of both mother and child. I very highly recommend this book if you wish to learn alternative and effective skills and strategies of parenting while continuing to having an impact on others."

~ Doris Muna ~
Mom, Healer, Founder of
Dorothea Essences, Author of
The Triangle of Health:
Discover Your Healing Journey

"This heartwarming book inspired me with a whole new possibility for my relationship with my children. Amanda models so beautifully something I have wondered about for a long time – how to share myself and my journey authentically with my children, in a way that keeps us deeply connected and helps us all to grow. As a transformational coach and facilitator, I've had the sense that my parenting could be as much an expression of my true purpose and potential as my professional work – if not more so. But I hadn't figured out how to translate all the lessons I've learned and skills I've grown into being the kind of mother I'd like to be for my kids. Amanda's story has given me new hope and many ideas for how to contribute the best of myself and my unique gifts to my children. I am deeply grateful."

~ Sherri Lassila ~
Transformational Mommy,
Speaker, Coach, and CEO
of Purpose Tribe

Upside-Down Mommy

How a Caterpillar Transformed
One Mommy's Breakdown
into Breakthrough

Amanda Johnson

Upside-Down Mommy
How a Caterpillar Transformed One
Mommy's Breakdown into Breakthrough
Published by
True to Intention
Ontario, California
www.TrueToIntention.com

Cover & Interior Illustration by Christopher Gomez
Cover Design by Dan Mulhern Design
Interior Design by Dawn Teagarden

ISBN: 978-0-9887809-1-0 (paperback)

Printed in the United States of America

www.TrueToIntention.com

To My Little Caterpillar…

May you never forget who you really are…

Acknowledgments

"I'm going to write and produce the book, and make it a bestseller, in less than six months."

Some would say I was crazy, but I knew it was possible when my family, my team, and my community didn't flinch, doubt, or question before asking, "How can I help?"

How blessed am I? Let me count the ways...

To the Divine Eyes and Hands that have unconditionally loved and supported me, and worked generously on my behalf, even when I couldn't see.

To My Family...

To my not-so-little-anymore caterpillar son Aaron, for not only being the motivation for my journey and my favorite teacher in this life, but for being my biggest cheerleader through the writing of this book and the development of the bestseller campaign. You always inspire me to "Girl-Up" and play bigger, and live inside the limitless question of "Why not?"

To my amazing husband Ryan, for believing in me, for trusting me, and for holding down the home front with so much love and support, so that I could take the time and space needed to not only write this, but to walk back through the darkness and heal the parts that still needed love. Revisiting some of our darkest days reminded me of how far we have come. I'm glad we didn't give up on Love or Us. You're still the one…

To my wonderful parents, for modeling the "I'm going to give my children a happier and healthier experience" intention. You absolutely did it. I honor and love you for laying a firm foundation of faith in miracles beneath me when I was young, for keeping me in your prayers when you didn't know how else to help me, for loving me through it all, and for now standing witness to the dream that was always meant to be for me. What more could a "best girl" ask for?

To my beautiful siblings, for your love and support. Chase, many of our long talks (okay, rants!) helped me to clarify and reshape the way I shared the concepts in this book. Thank you for being willing to engage and learn and let go of what doesn't make sense, and giving me the space to do the same. Ciara, you were the first baby in my life to prove that we all come to this world with purpose and we can choose to live it or not. Thank you for holding this dream with me, for listening to the promptings to pray and check in with me during the writing process, and for sharing your incredible energy and editing skills to make this book more powerful. Alyssa, that moment rocking you to sleep and hearing that still, small voice on the kitchen floor when I was sixteen became my anchor and north star when I felt lost. Thank you for always being a reminder of the unconditional love of God, and for caring about the details of this book as much as I do. I love you all...

To Grandma, for being a key part of this journey. If not for you and your support, I don't know how long it would have taken us. Thank you for believing in me, for reminding me to take care of myself, and for being an important part of my wing training.

To All of My Past and Present Teachers, Mentors, and Coaches...

To those who saw and nurtured my spirit in elementary and high school, thank you for your love and support. Mr. Larsen, I thought of you while I wrote the sixth chapter because you were one of the few who encouraged me to get really quiet and listen.

To Dr. Reynolds, for taking a chance and inviting me into the honors program, for asking the question that changed my life (What if it's not true?), and for then giving me the answer to every question that came after: "If you were to look — *really look* — through the eyes and into the soul of another person, you would be tempted to worship them." I wondered if it was blasphemy at the time, but now I understand. It's the divine image in all of us that loves, reflects, and heals.

To Alisa, for mentoring me, for believing in me when I didn't believe in myself, and for asking the question that called my purpose to re-emerge.

To Lisa, for creating the safe space for me to speak my truth, fall apart, and begin to heal myself. You called it "oxygen," but it was really my divine connection that I was missing, and it was you and your community through which "God became flesh" and loved me into my healing and a renewed connection. Thank you for saying 'yes' to being the vessel.

To Tia and Ahmondra, for not giving up on me, for modeling unconditional love and safety (no matter how I tested the safety of the space), and for seeing me healed and in my purpose before I could...for being my sisters on the journey.

To Ursula, for regularly asking, "So when are you gonna write that book?" and for giving me the safe space to call you and quit when I feel upside-down. "Okay, Amanda, what else would you do?" That question not only makes me laugh, it reminds me to go back to my BIG WHY. Thank you for being a model of living in one's purpose abundantly and with integrity, and for coaching me into flow and ease in my business. What would I do without you!?!

To Doris, for sharing your gift of healing with me, and helping me to heal the beliefs that were limiting my life emotionally, physically, relationally, and financially. There is no doubt you were placed on my path at the perfect time.

To Leeza, for helping me to heal my body, and for giving me a place to get quiet and reconnect.

To My Team...

To Christopher Gomez, for capturing my vision for the front cover and all of the other illustrations in this book. You are so incredibly talented. Thank you for doing this project from your heart, and for being curious about the broken wing.

To Dan Mulhern, for always opening the emails titled "You're gonna love me," for designing all of the online and offline graphics for my business from your heart, and for patiently working through the quick expansions and transformations True to Intention has already experienced. Thank you for taking Christopher's artwork and running with it to design a breath-taking book cover.

To Dawn Teagarden, for doing such a phenomenal job with the interior design of the book. It's even more beautiful than I dreamed.

To Jenee Dana, for holding all of the logistics for the book for me, and for holding the intention for ease and flow in the process. I don't think I could have gotten it to print without you — definitely not in the timeframe we did it.

To Kathy Sparrow, Lauren Hirchag, Ciara Coelho, and Alyssa Coelho, for making sure it was powerful and polished enough to go to print. Your coaching and editing gifts are a blessing to me, to my business, and to all of my clients. Thank you!

To My Cocoon-munity...

To Tami, for feeling the power of this message, and for being the midwife of this book — the first person I trusted to review each chapter and give me honest feedback. Thank you for turning my training on me and helping me to stay true to my intention, and for talking me off the ledge when the dark flashbacks made it hard to see.

To Kate, for being my comrade and walking with me through my dark night of the soul, for loving me unconditionally, and for helping me to remember the necessary details from that dark time while I was writing the book.

To the True to Intention Cocoon-munity — colleagues, partners, messengers, souls sisters and brothers, and friends — there are no words to express my gratitude. For the first half of my life, I felt "out of place" and longed for the type of safety, transparency, and purpose-sharing that we are experiencing in this community. Thank you for holding the space for me on this crazy amazing journey I call Impact!

With All My Love and Gratitude,

Contents

Prologue

How Can I Make Sure He Doesn't Forget?

"Happy birthday to you! Happy birthday to you!

Happy birthday, dear Amanda…Happy birthday to you!"

As if on ironic cue, the sun's last rays of the day disappeared from the room, and I strained to see the faces of those who raised their voice in celebration of my life.

Everyone was there. Family. Friends. Mentors. Teachers. Clients. Colleagues. They had all shown up for this very special birthday party, and my heart ached for them as they struggled to hold back tears and not allow their voices to crack with emotion.

They are trying so hard to hide the grief that has already set in.

I intentionally made eye contact with each person there and tried to let them know without words that it was okay for them to feel sad…and that I loved them and was grateful they had been in my life.

As the song concluded, I reached the end of the large circle and smiled at them. My guys.

I let the tears fall as I looked into my husband's eyes and

quietly thanked him for sharing his life and love with me, for being my best friend and my lover, for not giving up on us through the hard times, for keeping me grounded and honest, and for raising our beautiful son with me.

I shifted my gaze to the last one in the circle. *My sweet son. My angel.*

We smiled at each other through the tears, and then he moved closer and rested his head on my lap the way he had done a million times. I could almost hear his thoughts — "I need Mommy time!" — the words he always used to let me know he needed a snuggle.

They are trying so hard to hide the grief that has already set in.

Sweet Boy. I ran my fingers through his hair. *How could I ever put into words how your presence in my life has changed me? How could I make you understand how you helped me heal my heart and taught me the most important lessons I have ever learned as I tried to figure out how to parent you without limiting you?*

Everyone in the room must have seen our interaction and decided to give us some time.

Feeling my lap dampen with his tears, I rubbed his back and wondered…

The dream was so real, so intense, that I woke in a puddle of tears.

How can I make sure he doesn't forget who he really is and has already been to me, especially through the grief of losing me?

And almost as soon as I finished asking the question, I knew the answer.

I'll write him letters, give them to Ryan, and ask him to share one every year on my birthday...

The dream was so real, so intense, that I woke in a puddle of tears. I kissed my husband gently on the cheek, slipped out of bed, and quietly tiptoed to my son's room.

"Mommy?" his little voice sounded confused.

"Yes, Big Man. It's me. I'm here. I just needed some Big Man time." I pulled myself onto his top bunk and snuggled up next to him.

When I knew he had fallen back to sleep, I let the tears flow again.

"How can I make sure he doesn't forget?" The words echoed through my mind.

I'm not even sick, let alone dying. Why did I have that dream?

I watched his chest rise and fall, and listened to his sweet little sleep sounds.

What would I say to him if I knew I only had a year left?

What would I leave for him to remember who he is?

What would I apologize for?

Gulp. The tears flowed harder as I remembered the one moment I knew I could never take back...

Introduction

We Don't Intend to Damage Them...

It was a long morning. You know, one of those that make you want to crawl back in bed. Everything took longer than it should have, and everyone in the house was a little crankier than normal. Yet, I was determined to take my little guy to the store for some much-needed new clothes. I put my tired smile in place and headed out, intending to get back in time for his nap.

The more he struggled... the more desperately I wrestled him... and the harder I spanked.

I raced through the store to find clothes I could afford and was just stepping into line when I heard his small voice, "Mommy, I wan' dat..." I turned to see him pointing at a cute stuffed dog sitting near the register.

My heart sunk.

"Sweetie, I didn't plan on getting that doggy today. Maybe we can get it next time we come to this store." The shame attached to the words seared my tongue on their way out. *What kind of life am I going to be able to give this child? I can't even afford a small stuffed animal!* As I felt the pain erupt, I lowered my voice, as if hoping to keep the shame of my situation from oozing all over me, my son, and the people waiting patiently in line behind me.

With tired eyes, my angel looked up and pleaded, "Mommy, pleeeaaaase."

"No, Honey. I didn't plan to do that today. I *can't* do that today." Forcing back the angry tears, I paid for the clothes while his no-nap-tantrum escalated.

His tired whimpers turned to exhausted sobs, and all of my efforts to distract him failed. His stuffed animals, cookies, toys — nothing worked. When he began to scream, it took all of my focus not to scream back. I took a deep breath and ran out the doors of the store, rapidly approaching my wit's end.

By the time the doors closed behind me, it was over. Years of piled up disappointment, anger, and shame that had been quietly boiling beneath the surface took over.

I have hazy memories of grabbing him at his elbow and dragging him across the parking lot to the car, throwing the bag of clothes in the back of the car, and then picking him up and hurling him into his seat with far too much force. The more he struggled to get away from his crazed mom, the more desperately I wrestled him into the seat...

and the harder I spanked. I remember yelling, but the words still escape my memory. All I can remember is the feeling of being completely out of control…and then his horrified expression.

It was at that moment, when I witnessed the undeniable terror and lack of recognition in his eyes that I crumbled. I landed across the back seat with my head on his lap. The rush of shame caused me such intense physical pain that I cried out and buried my face in my hands as the tears erupted. *Oh my God, what have I done?!? I promised him that I would protect him from everything and everyone that would limit him. And look at what I've done!*

"Mommy?" he asked through his own tears, wondering if the monster had left.

"Big Man, I'm so sorry…"

And then he broke my heart into smaller pieces as he gently caressed my hair and face while I cried out the pain and apologized over and over again, wondering if I would ever find a way to undo what I had just done.

Have you ever lost control with your child?
Said or done something you later regretted, and
wondered if you have done irreparable damage?

It took me three years (and a very safe and sacred space) to
tell another soul about my shameful behavior that day, but
it only took me moments to grasp the beginning of the
most profound truth I have ever learned about parenting
and about life — the truth that I desire to share with other
parents through this book.

You see, up until that moment in the parking lot, I was a
"rather exceptional parent," especially for being so young;
and anyone who knew me during that time would testify
to that end because I had been well-prepared for the
parenting business.

But in one moment, on a bad day, I nearly crushed his soul
and spirit.

As I laid there on his lap, I wondered where I had gone
wrong. *I didn't mean to damage him.* In fact, I had gone
above and beyond to integrate all of my training into my
parenting approach and style.

And yet, I had forgotten a truth that had been reinforced repeatedly through my education: *Children follow models, not concepts.*

And the rest of my life was a mess. That day, besides this sweet little two-year-old angel of mine, I felt I had nothing to live for. I had lost my husband to depression and my happily-ever-after to "reality," I had lost my religion and my community with it, and I had lost all hope that I'd ever earn more than "never enough to get by."

Suddenly, it seemed that I was at the center of a divine intervention.

All the training, tools, and skills I have acquired through my experience, my education, and my teacher training won't do a damn bit of good if I don't figure out how to heal my own life. Filling him with the right affirmations and facilitating his own wisdom won't be enough if one of the people he loves most in the world is broken enough to completely lose control the way I just did.

I cannot teach my son how to live a happy and healthy life if I, myself, am depressed and sick. I cannot expect him to grow up and love his work if he witnesses me hating mine. I cannot expect to help him live life without limits if I do not learn how to remove mine and show him that it's possible. I have to heal my life... but how?

That moment in the parking lot catalyzed a journey of healing for me, and the most phenomenal journey with my son. That journey is the one I want to share with you in the pages of this book.

Still disconnected, alone, and depressed, I became a desperate seeker, determined to find a way to heal my life and give my son a better model to follow. In between play time and my other responsibilities, I read books and watched movies that promised to show me how I could heal my life. I learned about energy, limiting beliefs, and the power of words and feelings. It was crazy how "the next book I needed" always dropped off of the bookstore shelf, and how "the right people" began to show up in my life — people who could somehow see past the plastic smile, the pain, and the limitations, and remind me who I really am.

Suddenly, it seemed that I was at the center of a divine intervention, where everything and everyone that crossed my path appeared to do so with divine intention. Every experience brought insight...because I was looking for it. Everyone and every experience became my teacher... because I allowed them to be.

> *And I know, that like me, you are at the center of a divine intervention...*

And then, one day, while playing in the garden with my son, I realized that I was not alone at the center of a divine intervention. Still living without limits, he was everyday proof to me that happiness, fearlessness, unconditional love, and playfulness are our natural state. And then the craziest thought crossed my mind: *Maybe he is MY model — leading ME back into my natural state of joy, abundance, and no limits.*

This is the journey I want to share with you — the journey of my son, the teacher, reminding me who I really am and inspiring and empowering me to live a life without limits.

This book is written as a series of letters to my son, capturing the lessons he taught me, in hopes that he will never forget who he really is — a soul with purpose, power, and access to any possibility. And I pray that as he grows and faces his own challenges in life, he will find this book again and be reminded of who he really is and who he has been to me already.

And…this book has also been written for you — the parent of another beautiful soul.

If you are reading this book, I am certain that you care deeply about your child or children. I know that you are doing your very best to raise them. I know that you have probably found yourself in moments reminiscent of mine in the parking lot — maybe not to that extreme (or maybe it was worse) — but you know you have done some damage. I know the guilt and shame. I know you would give everything you have to undo it. I know that your heart aches with love and the desire to see them grow up to be happy and healthy and powerful. *I am not a parenting expert or a psychologist. And I am not a perfect parent.* And I know that some days, you feel like you have no idea what you are doing or how to help them get there.

And I know, that like me, you are at the center of a divine intervention...

It is no coincidence that you have picked up this book. It is no coincidence that you were at that one place where that one person mentioned it. It is no coincidence that they were made aware of the book and read it when they did.

And the person before them... And, well, you get the picture...

This book is about my son and me, but it's really about a new way of approaching the parenting process. I call this new approach *The Butterfly Approach* because, as you will see throughout the book, I had the most profound *ahas*, about parenting and about life, over the course of a two-week period, as I sat still and witnessed caterpillar larvae transform into caterpillars and then butterflies. Each phase of the butterfly process taught or reminded me of a lesson (or two, or three, or many), and what unfolded was a philosophy of parenting and living that has completely transformed my life and become the framework of transformation that I use to help my child and others (authors, parents, etc.) on their journey of discovering and owning who they really are — of becoming *true to intention*.

Your relationship with your child and your life will never be the same.

My prayer is that you will begin reading this book, knowing that you have been invited into a sacred space to get something and take it back with you into your parenting and your life. I am not a parenting expert or a psychologist. And I am *not* a perfect parent. I still get it wrong sometimes. I still say and do disempowering things regularly because I am still on the journey. I am still healing. I have just found a way — an approach — that allows me to live inside of a safe and sacred space with my son and clean things up as quickly as I mess them up. At the end of the day, I am just a mom who wants to share a profound insight with other moms (and dads too!) because it changed my life.

There *are* tools, skills, and strategies woven into the stories, simply because I was using them, and while I'm not going to point to them and say, "This is a strategy," I know you will see the ones you need to see. When one reveals itself to you, make a note in the book or journal it, and then make a commitment to use it that day or the next time a similar situation arises in your relationship. But don't stress if you don't see them. The purpose of this book is really to share the philosophy, the underlying principles, that guide my approach to every interaction with my son and, now, everyone else in my life.

So, take your time. It may look like a small book, but it's packed. It's better to take your time and let yourself really absorb the stories, everything that is happening inside of them, and the truths they are meant to whisper to you as you read.

And, I want to warn you that you may get emotional as you read it, not just because you are witnessing the love of a parent and child relationship, or a powerful healing journey, but because you will likely see parts of you and your parenting process that you would rather ignore. But I want to encourage you... When you want to close the book, chuck it across the room, or throw it away because something in here triggers feelings of sadness, anger, powerlessness, shame, or regret, those are the moments of opportunity for your own transformation. When those feelings start to bubble, take a deep breath and give yourself your own sacred space. No matter what you said and did, you didn't know what you didn't know...

And now you will...

And your relationship with your child and your life will never be the same.

1
Magic Eggs

"You are a child of God.

Your playing small does not serve the world.
There's nothing enlightened about
shrinking so that other people won't
feel insecure around you.
We were born to make manifest the
glory of God that is within us.
It's not just in some of us;
it's in everyone."

Marianne Williamson

"Big Man, look what came in the mail today!" Having run from the mailbox, I took a deep breath to cool the burning in my chest as I continued to run toward the kitchen to open the box.

"The caterpillars?" It wasn't even two seconds before I heard the sweet sound of your quick three-year-old footsteps on the tile, following my voice to the kitchen.

We'd purchased the Butterfly Bungalow and sent the card requesting the eggs almost two weeks earlier, and both of us had eagerly run to the mailbox every day to see if they'd arrived. The day they came, I'd decided to check the mail while you were finishing an episode of Blue's Clues.

I grabbed the razor blade to cut through the tape and noticed my hands were shaking. *Why am I so excited about these butterflies? I guess it's going to be fun to watch him witness the metamorphosis. It will be like magic.*

Smiling to myself, I remembered your puzzled look in the garden almost a year before. You'd been chasing a sweet little butterfly while I rested my aching body on the steps. When I decided to go in the house to refill my water bottle, something caught my eye as I approached the door.

Forgetting the pain I was in, I bent down and saw a little caterpillar crawling on a potted plant. *Oh, this will be fun.*

"Caterpillars are baby butterflies. This little guy is going to turn into a butterfly like the one you were just chasing."

"Aaron, look what I found!" You came running over.

"What's dat?" you said as you fixed your eyes on the fuzzy creature I was holding.

"Can you say 'ca-ter-pil-lar'?" I slowed my speech so you could hear every sound.

"Ca-pil-er!" You couldn't get the word out fast enough.

I giggled at your excited attempt to say it. "Yes. Caterpillars are baby butterflies. This little guy is going to turn into a butterfly like the one you were just chasing."

The look on your face was priceless. Your big brown eyes got even bigger. I could see you trying to make sense of what I'd just said, but after a few attempts at explaining, I realized that at two years old, you were unable to imagine such a transformation.

That's why I was so excited to find the Butterfly Bungalow at the store.

It's time for us to witness one of the most amazing transformations that take place in nature. How do eggs become caterpillars and then butterflies?

As I pulled the container out of the box, I wrote my shaking hands off as excitement for you, but now I know that my spirit was leaping with joy *for me.*

You could hardly contain yourself as you watched me open the box and pull out the little container full of butterfly eggs. I handed it to you and watched the confusion cross your face as you peered into it. "Mommy, where are the caterpillars?"

"Well, Honey. It looks like they sent us some magic eggs."

"Magic eggs?"

"Yes, pretty soon, just like magic, you'll see little caterpillars come out of those little eggs."

"Magic eggs…" Your voice trailed off as you stared into the little container, unwilling to divert your eyes and miss the magic your mommy had promised was going to take place.

And so our journey began…

Arriving with Purpose

"Hey, Little Man. It's nice to meet you." Your daddy touched your cheek and said the words I'd been unable to find as I looked into your eyes. After a few minutes, he asked the question we'd been debating for months, "So, what do you think? Is he an Aaron or an Aidan?" He leaned over my head to get a better look at your face.

Yes, Aaron is the perfect name. It means Enlightened One, and…

"I think he's Aaron. Look at his eyes. It's like he knows something we don't know. Doesn't he look like he's already here on a mission?" I looked up at your daddy for confirmation. When he smiled and nodded, I looked back at you and asked, "Why are you here, Little Man? What are you here to do in the world?"

What if you are here on a mission and have something BIG to be, to give, to do in this world?

This question formed the foundation of our relationship and deepened my commitment to protect you from the pain and limitations that I'd experienced and was still experiencing when you were born.

I will do everything I can to help you do what you came here to do.

"Mommy, what is *praying*?" Your three-year-old voice was curiously eager.

I paused for a minute and then finished pulling the blankets up to your chin before answering, "Ummmm… why do you ask, Sweetie?" You'd caught me completely off-guard. Both of us still in the middle of working out our individual spiritual crises, your daddy and I had agreed to leave the 'God conversation' alone until you asked, and we felt capable of having the conversation.

He's only three! Really? Already? What am I going to tell him?

"I heard Aunt Megan talk about praying with Chris last night. What is *praying*?"

"Well, Big Man…" I stammered through an explanation that most people in this world believe in a God that is watching over all of us on earth, and that praying is a way to thank Him for taking care of us and to ask Him for help when we get stuck.

"I want to pray!" You almost screamed it with excitement, and I smiled, hoping to hide my terror.

How long has it been since I've prayed?

"Okay, go ahead. I'll stay right here with you."

"Okay, Mommy. " You closed your eyes and started, "Dear God…" There was a long pause, and I lifted my head to look up at you. You were staring straight at me, as if you didn't want to interrupt *me*.

"Now what, Mommy?"

"Oh, yes. Right. You've never done this before." I took a long deep breath before answering, "Well, most people start with a 'Thank you' list. You can thank God for whatever you are thankful for."

Closing your eyes, you started again, "Dear God, thank you for my mommy and daddy. Thank you for this house. Thank you for yummy food. Thank you for Grandma and Papa and Grammy and my aunts and…"

Your gratitude list was very long, and the tears quietly rolled down my face. *I guess we do have quite a bit to be thankful for.* I silently added to your list: I'd found some books that were helping me understand why I was experiencing such emotional and physical pain and that I could heal it, so I was feeling hopeful again; I'd just been offered a writing instruction job that I could do from home, so I could stay home with you and start to make some money; and I'd just been introduced to a really amazing woman who'd asked me to help her with her book about intentional selling.

"Mommy?" I hadn't noticed that you had stopped and were looking at me again.

"Yes?" I quickly wiped my tears away and looked up at you.

"Now what?" Your big eyes and smile made me giggle.

"Well, now people usually ask for help with stuff they can't figure out how to do on their own. If they are sick, they pray for help getting healthy. If they..." I tried to give examples that would make sense to you.

"Okay." Again, closing your eyes, "Dear God, please help all of the little kids in the world who don't have mommies and daddies. Please help all the people who are sick to feel better. Please help everyone to be loved..."

> *"Dear God, please help all of the little kids in the world who don't have mommies and daddies. Please help all the people who are sick to feel better. Please help everyone to be loved..."*

For the first time in years, I felt the presence of God in our home, and the dam in my heart broke open as I realized that I not only didn't need to worry about you developing a connection with God in spite of my crisis (you were clearly already connected!) but that you'd just made my questions about doctrine and philosophy pointless.

This is spirituality and connection with God in its purest form. This…I am willing to participate in.

"Mommy?"

I wiped away more tears and took a breath to steady my voice. "Yes, Big Man."

"Am I done?"

"I don't know. Do you have anything else to say?"

"No, I'm sleepy." You rubbed your eyes to make your point.

"Well then, I think your prayer was perfect." Gently pushing the hair away from your eyes, I caressed your cheek, kissed you goodnight, and walked out of your room, weeping and praying for the first time in years, *Dear God, thank you for sending me this angel. Thank you for the hope that it can be this simple. Please help me to heal my life.*

Everything You Need

Your prayer was the final answer to questions that had begun to form in me as I spent time with you.

What if you are here on a mission and have something BIG to be, to give, to do in this world? What if all I have to do is discover it with you — to nurture, protect, and honor the purpose and value in you until you can do it on your own? Wouldn't that mean that you have (or have access to) everything you need to become what you are meant to become?

The more I entertained the possibility that you had everything you needed, and I didn't need to mold or train you, the more you confirmed it. Physically, emotionally, and mentally, you were always the one to tell me when you needed something, and when you didn't. You pushed your food away when you were full and laid down when you were tired. You knew when you were ready to crawl and walk, and all I had to do was keep helping you see the possibilities.

What if all I have to do is discover it with you — to nurture, protect, and honor the purpose and value in you until you can do it on your own?

You yanked on my shirt and said, "Up," or "Mommy, look at me," when you needed affection or wanted my undivided attention.

I had begun to entertain the idea that this could be what our entire relationship was supposed to be like. Physically, emotionally, and now even spiritually, you were engaged in a natural process of growth and already had what you needed for the next phase, and maybe my job (like ours with the magic eggs) was to nurture, protect, honor, and enjoy what was unfolding, and to always inspire the possibility of MORE. (Oh, and to learn from it.)

The Alternative

"Mom, do you remember when I found you hiding in the kitchen, crying? Why were you crying?"

Shocked, I dropped my fork and stared at you. "Aaron, that was four years ago. You weren't even two yet. You remember that?"

"Yes. Why were you crying?" You kept eating your lunch, but fixed your gaze on me.

I knew there was no way to get out of this. I had to tell the truth. "Well, I was very sad back then, and I was crying to let some of the sad out."

"Why were you *so* sad? You were *really* crying."

Oh dear. How am I going to explain this?

I stammered through an explanation that I thought you would understand at five years old: I was having trouble at work, I was sad that a few people in my life were unhappy and being unkind, and I was also feeling sick in my body.

But Kiddo, that was the kid version, and I think it's important for you to know the adult version…

Kiddo, that was the kid version, and I think it's important for you to know the adult version.

Remember *Percival, The Plain Little Caterpillar?* I found that book in a craft store when you were two years old. I read it before purchasing — you know how I am about choosing the right messages! — and started to cry in the middle of the store. Little Percival was very, very plain, but living in a world full of color. The garden was full of insects and creatures that were rich with color, and he admired every one of them while wondering to himself why he was so plain. Eventually, he felt sad and tired, so he wrapped himself up for a good sleep and began to dream about colors. Miraculously, when he woke up, he had every one of the colors he had admired on the other creatures painted on his own beautiful wings.

The tears had come because *I was Percival*. It was a time in my life when I felt so "different," like I didn't belong anywhere. Everyone else my age seemed to be moving forward and making their life work while I was losing one dream after another and watching my life take on more and more shades of grey. I had acquired my teaching credential but walked away from that dream because the system was broken, and I didn't feel strong enough to fight or fix it. I was scared that I had wasted my education, and unsure about how to provide for our little family. Your daddy and I could not get on the same page as hard as we tried. My poor parents, siblings, and friends had no idea why I was so sad and tired. And, at the ripe age of twenty-five, a doctor told me that if I didn't figure out how to deal with all of my anger and pain, my fibromyalgia symptoms (achiness, pain, fatigue, weight gain, etc.) would get worse and paralyze me by the time I turned thirty.

> *I felt like all of my reasons for living and loving were disappearing...*

Honestly, I felt like all of my reasons for living and loving were disappearing...

The only light and color and purpose in my life was YOU — my little caterpillar, who had entered my life at just the right moment and become a constant reminder that the message of Percival was true and real:

We all really do come into this world with what we need to become who we are meant to be (artists, dancers, teachers, authors, healers, partners, parents, etc.), but most of us, not knowing what the final design looks like, get caught up with what we see, or what we are encouraged to focus upon.

And that is where my pain was *really* coming from.

It wasn't that all of those bad things were happening, it was that *I felt powerless* to do anything about them. I had forgotten that I also was born with a magic egg — a divine spirit that had innate value and purpose to give to the world and that knew how to connect with God and change and heal my life — because I had not been encouraged to focus on and listen to it.

I had grown up in a small rural area, surrounded by nature and lots of

I had forgotten that I also was born with a magic egg — a divine spirit that had innate value and purpose to give to the world and that knew how to connect with God and change and heal my life.

people who loved me dearly. Grammy and Papa showed me that they loved me and often told me they were proud of me. They even sent me to a school where I was surrounded by people who held the same values of love, integrity, and kindness. This small private school quickly became my second home.

I knew nothing else growing up, and I didn't question the message.

Because it was a Christian school, every subject was taught through the lens of Christianity. Science was the history of God's creation, and History was the story of God's many attempts to redeem His creation that had gone astray. Between my regular subjects, additional Bible classes, chapel times, Sunday school classes, and eventually youth groups, I was literally saturated with the message of salvation. In fact, by the time I was ten years old, I was determinedly converting all of my friends and family with that message, "You are a sinner, but God still loves you and wants to save you from your sin. Ask Him into your heart, and you will be saved."

I knew nothing else growing up, and I didn't question the message. The people I love the most believed it wholeheartedly, and there was no reason to think differently. I just kept receiving it: "You are a sinner, Amanda, saved by grace. Without God, you can do no good thing."

My community had unknowingly and unintentionally "programmed" me to be obsessed with the "sin nature" — constantly trying to save myself, and the people I loved so dearly, from it.

It's all I saw, so when I was seven years old and the mother of one of my friends said, "You cannot play with my daughter anymore because you make her feel bad," and I had no memory of doing anything wrong, I just assumed it was because of this brokenness — this sin nature inside of me. I made her, and soon others, feel bad without any specific action to point to (or try to change). This "sin nature" started to separate and isolate me from people I loved, and I felt powerless to change it.

By the time I understood that the reason for her being upset was that I got straight As while she was struggling for Cs, it was too late. The damage had already been done, and all this new information helped me to do was to more intentionally hide part of my magic egg from the world... because it seemed to make others feel bad? I was isolated, alone, hurting, and sure that it was because there was something wrong with me — something I couldn't change.

It wasn't until my freshman year that we started to hear a slightly different message and witness a different type of Christianity. We'd found a church that was pretty untraditional, and it was there that I witnessed miracles. I saw people healed — as a result of *my* prayers. I saw money manifest for God's work, and *I* was an active participant.

The message of being a sinner saved by grace was still present, but the focus shifted to "doing God's work." Here, the people of God were powerful when they stayed in alignment with God's purpose for their lives, which was, in Jesus' words, "to do greater things than these (the miracles He had done)" — to take care of the poor and needy, heal the sick, and love everyone with HIS love. The focus was no longer on me being a sinner, but on me being a vessel for His Work.

It was there that I witnessed miracles.

I was feeling pretty good by the time I graduated and headed off to the university. Your daddy had asked me to marry him, and I'd said *'yes'* to him. I'd also been accepted to the honors program at the university. When the director of the honors program called to tell me about the program, I pushed through the terror of taking on such a rigorous intellectual process and said *'yes'* to strengthening my faith so that I could be a stronger vessel.

I had no idea what I had signed up for. This program was designed to help me make my beliefs and faith *my own*, which meant that it began by challenging every "truth" I had learned at home and in school.

"Why do you believe that?" The first time I heard the question, all I could say was, "It's what I was taught." And then I watched my world fall apart as I asked the next logical question: *What if it's not true, or the whole truth?*

The process was painful. At times, it felt as though my whole world was coming apart at the seams, and I felt anger...so much anger. I was furious with everyone who had "thought for me" while I was growing up. I know now that they were all doing the very best they knew how, and that it was a heck of a lot better than what they'd experienced as kids; but back then, I was just angry and determined to make my beliefs *my own*.

Fortunately, I focused most of my fury on helping other young people avoid the pain that I was experiencing, and as far as I could tell, the best way to do that was to start asking them to think for themselves while they were still young. (Sound familiar?) At the end of my first semester, my initial dream of becoming a journalist who inspired young people in their faith gave way to the dream of becoming a teacher who said, "It's okay to ask questions, and it's okay to not have the answers at first. The important thing is that you get used to asking yourself the questions, so that you are the one finding the answers for your own life."

What if it's not true, or the whole truth?

My previous experience had taught me one thing for sure: There is a God, and He loves us unconditionally. So if we truly believe in a loving God, then we can trust that when we ask for truth, He will reveal it to us, right?

As I began my teacher-credentialing program, I found myself fascinated with the self-image literature and the theories and insight *my* father was beginning to share with me. No doubt the fascination was rooted in my new focus of figuring out who I was and what I thought about myself and the world, and helping young people do the same, but the self-image conversation became central to all of my studies.

"Children rise and fall to the expectations placed on them," so I would have to be careful to keep the bar high.

"We can only accomplish what we believe we can accomplish," so I would have to believe in the child's ability and let them borrow my belief in them until they believed for themselves.

"One's self-image and belief in their abilities are largely shaped by the adults and circumstances of their life," so I better be careful with my words and avoid placing additional limitations on them. My words have power.

"The self-image can only be changed through repetition of a new experience/ truth about oneself," so if I wanted to help these already limited self-images lose their limits, I had to give them enough successful moments that they would begin to expect those successes more than the failures.

By the end of my college years, between the teacher-credentialing program and my dad's mentoring and training in transforming a self-image, I had discovered and was using some powerful tools and skills to help people replace their old self-images with new, more powerful ones. One of my best friends used these tools to overcome her alcoholism almost overnight, and another handicapped friend overcame a number of her physical handicaps once she realized that they were limits imposed by her self-image rather than her true physical condition.

Now all I had to do was figure out how to change my own self-image from simply a "sinner saved by grace" to "a powerful vessel for the Work."

It was easier said than done. All of my limited "sinner-focused" thinking and unresolved anger had created some horribly difficult circumstances in my life. Physically, I was almost crippled with achiness, pain, and exhaustion. Emotionally, I felt isolated, alone, and angry with myself for pushing everyone away and not knowing how to restore the relationships. Financially, I was broke and too exhausted to work inside of a broken education system. And spiritually, I was still trying to figure out how to reconnect. I'd spent the past four years working through questions in my head, not knowing how to express or work through the pain in my heart.

> *Now all I had to do was figure out how to change my own self-image from simply a "sinner saved by grace" to "a powerful vessel for the Work."*

And that, sweet boy, is what you were born into.

When I saw you arrive with such obvious purpose and *no* limits, I promised you that I would protect you from everything that had limited me...

I promised to focus on the divine in you — the magic egg — that holds everything you need to be, do, and give all you are meant to be, give, and do.

I promised to allow you to *become*, and to honor the natural growth process that had begun in my womb.

I promised to stay in a place of curiosity and reflection instead of teaching, training, and molding you into something I (or our culture) would deem successful.

I promised to learn how to be a powerful witness to your life, to affirm your worth and value, and to reflect back all of your divine qualities, talents, and gifts as you expressed them…to help *you* see that you have everything you need.

And that, sweet boy, is what you were born into.

I promised to help you avoid and reshape unhealthy habits and to expose you to as many possibilities as I could.

I promised you I wouldn't limit you, and I used every skill, tool, and strategy I had.

But that day in the parking lot — when I lost my mind on you because of all of my limitations and the anger, shame, and pain they caused — I realized that at some point, I had to find, focus on, and love my own magic egg.

But how?

Well, you guided me to the answer to that question too…

2
Caterpillar Craze

"Children confront us with our paradoxes and hypocrisies, and we are exposed. You need to find an answer for every why. Why do we do this? Why don't we do that? — and often there isn't a good one. So you say, simply, because. Or you tell a story that you know isn't true. And whether or not your face reddens, you blush. The shame of parenthood — which is a good shame — is that we want our children to be more whole than we are, to have satisfactory answers."

Jonathan Safran Foer

"Mommy, co'mere! Hurry!"

I ran to the kitchen, not wanting to miss whatever had you so excited.

"What is it, Big Man? What's happening?"

"Look! The caterpillars came out of the magic eggs!"

"How exciting!" I smiled, enjoying the awe-inspired wonder on your face more than the sight of the little caterpillars.

"They're so little."

"Yes, they are. But they're going to grow. See how they are running around eating all that food in the jar?"

You nodded.

"Pretty soon, they will be really big."

"Can I give them a string cheese?" I had to hold back my laughter when you offered to share your favorite snack.

"No, Sweetie. They don't eat our food. They are supposed to eat leaves like the one that was in our garden. But it looks like whoever sent them to us gave them plenty of food in this jar."

We watched them run around and eat the jelly-like nutrients at the bottom of the jar.

"Mommy, they go *so* fast."

"You're right. They do move fast. I wonder where they are trying to go in such a hurry."

"Maybe they are REALLY hungry!"

"Well, speaking of hungry…how about we get you some breakfast and come back to check on the caterpillars later?"

"Okay," you agreed, reluctant to leave your little friends.

We had breakfast and then got distracted playing in the garden for a few hours, both of us completely forgetting about our fuzzy friends until right before dinner. You must have thought about them again while I was working at the stove.

"Mommy, look! Hurry!"

Your eyes were as big as your face as you held the jar out in my direction.

"What happened?"

"They are SO big!"

As I peered into the container, I caught my breath. They had nearly doubled in size.

"Wow, I didn't know they grew *that* fast."

"What's that? Poop?" You pointed to black stuff on the bottom of the jar.

"I don't know. It looks like some of their fuzzies came off. Maybe the first fuzzies weren't stretchy enough to grow with them."

We sat together and watched our fuzzy friends as they continued to move crazy fast, eating everything in their path.

Oh boy. I wonder when they will cocoon. I hope we're awake to see the process.

"Amanda, I think your autobiography is beautiful. I don't know how they could possibly say 'no' to you. All of your education and experience seems to have perfectly equipped you for this. And the way this all came about for you...it's divine." I smiled as I read this first part of Ursula's email.

She's right. It kinda shocked me while I was writing it. It really does look like every bit of my life experience and education has been orchestrated to prepare me for this work — like a Divine Set-up.

Aaron, our nightmare moment in the parking lot was a wake-up call. After the initial shock, anger, and "How could I have done this to my child?" depression wore off (it took months), I made a decision: *I have to find a way to heal my life.* I couldn't bear the thought of hurting you like that again. My desperate search began.

Too ashamed to talk to anyone about any of it, I went to the bookstore and found Louise Hay's book *You Can Heal Your Life*. Actually, it felt more like the book found me. As I walked through the self-improvement section, the book literally fell off the shelf and landed at my feet. Of course, I bought it and was surprised when it confirmed that doctor's insight — that all of my physical pain was simply the expression of my intense emotional pain, which was caused by the untrue beliefs I had about myself and God.

For example, my thyroid had quit working because I had stifled my expression and stopped asking for what *I* wanted. When my rage, sadness, or pain about my inability to have friends came up, I didn't use my voice to express it or ask for what I needed. The negativity got stuck there in my throat and began to hurt the organs and tissues nearby, eventually creating dis-ease in my body.

Whoa. I knew that what we believe about ourselves (self-image) defines our life experience — that we can only accomplish what we believe we can accomplish. And…I guess I knew that it could affect our bodies after working with the girl whose beliefs were creating more physical limitations than her disorder was. But I never imagined that emotional pain could create physical pain. Is it possible that all of my symptoms could go away if I healed the emotional pain?

Is it possible that all of my symptoms could go away if I healed the emotional pain?

Hungry for "the how," I devoured one book after another and even began using physical exercise to get the icky emotion *out* of my body. Remember the punching bag we put up in the back yard? Oh yeah — that helped! I also began using affirmations to replace some of the lies I'd begun to believe (i.e. "I can't tell others how I feel") with more truthful statements (i.e. "I can express my feelings honestly and ask for what I want").

A few things started to change. I felt less achy and began to really enjoy my work with Alisa's online writing instruction company. Of course, I was a little sad that it didn't take off the way we'd hoped, but looking back, I can see the divine hand at work in it. It was through her that I met Ursula — a soul sister who needed my help with her book, who helped me to remember the power of intention and belief, and then just happened to talk about this movie called *The Secret*.

I watched it and thought it was awesome, of course, and was grateful to already be on the journey of "changing my thinking and changing my life" — of using the Law of Attraction to my advantage. The more I focused on what I wanted, and my ability to attract it, the more the fog started to clear and possibilities became visible. It was a series of slow aha moments, until the day I found my magic egg…

> *It was a series of slow aha moments, until the day I found my magic egg…*

I'd previewed Alisa's book for her, and was telling her how sure I was that it would change people's lives when she asked a surprising question, "When are you going to write *your* book?" I laughed out loud, but winced inwardly. She had no idea that I had been suffering emotionally and physically — that I didn't believe I had anything to give to the world. *I am just trying to figure out how to feel better and survive.* Seeing that she'd hit a nerve, she asked one more question and then graciously said goodbye. Turning on my heel, I ran to the car, and cried all the way home, asking myself the last question she'd asked me, "What value do you have to give to the world right now?"

I don't know! I feel broken. Everything in my life is still a mess — my marriage, relationships, finances...all of it.

And then it hit me! The value I have to give...

The one thing I have done well, except for that horrible moment in the parking lot, is raise Aaron. Everyone has complimented me on how well-adjusted, sweet, and respectful he is. I know it's because I've been careful to focus on the Divine in him and reinforce his self-image, to speak powerful words and messages, and to allow him to grow and become who he is meant to be, like those little caterpillars we watched in the bungalow. Oh my goodness! I've been using the Law of Attraction with him, and I haven't known it! What if I could write a book for parents... and children...and...?

Aaron, I had uncovered my magic egg — the value I am meant to bring to the world — and activated that divine part of me that knew it was all possible...and meant to be.

By the time I got home (only forty-five minutes after Alisa had asked the question), I had mentally outlined seven books for parents and children, contacted an illustrator, and determined to attract a *Secret* Teacher to help me get this message to the masses.

> *Everyone except Ursula laughed in my face, as if to imply, "Who are you to do such a thing — to even think that it is possible?"*

Of course, over the next few weeks, I was fired up enough to not care that almost everyone I told about my idea (everyone except Ursula) laughed in my face, as if to imply, "Who are you to do such a thing — to even think that is possible?"

I know, but it just makes sense. Somehow, I know this is going to happen.

Three months (to the day) after I had uncovered my magic egg, set my intention for it, and started to act as if it was as good as done, *Secret* Teacher Lisa Nichols — through a series of too many crazy, synchronistic events to mention here — walked into a Sizzler behind us and invited me to her transformational workshop the following weekend.

Did I just do this?

I went to the workshop…and whew! I cried for eight hours straight! Somehow, I finally felt safe enough to express some of the pain out loud.

At the end of the day, when she offered the opportunity to become a facilitator for her transformational teen program, my heart leapt. *Yes, I need to learn how to do this! This is what I want to do with mommies and kids!* I ran to the back of the room, grabbed the application, and raced home to fill it out and figure out how the heck I was going to pay for the program.

One of their requests was that I write an autobiography, demonstrating why I was a good candidate for the program. I finished the autobiography and there was no one more fit to preview it than Ursula, the woman who had believed in my intention.

Pulling myself back from Memory Lane, I kept reading Ursula's email.

"And the part about Aaron...as I was reading it, I had this vision of him leading an army of angels to help you heal your life. It was so beautiful..."

I gasped for my next breath and let the tears flow.

What if he is here to help me? What if part of his purpose is to help me heal my life?

As I reflected on the possibility, a ton of moments flashed across my mind, as if to answer the question.

My Caterpillar Mirror

I spent long hours snuggled up with you on my chest when you were a baby, listening to your easy breathing and smelling your sweet breath. *I've never loved anyone like this. You are so sweet and…perfect.* Something inside of me longed to keep you there as long as I could — feeling love and connection with another person again. I was needed, wanted, and loved…unconditionally. I didn't feel like I had to ask, work, or manipulate to get it. It was just there, and it was healing me, gently reminding me of the moments I'd held one of my baby sisters and heard that still, small voice say, "You know how much you love that baby? It doesn't even come close to how much I love you. You know how you would never punish or send her away for making a mistake? I don't do that either."

What if he is here to help me? What if part of his purpose is to help me heal my life?

Being with you in your pure, limitless expression allowed me to begin to remember that mine was still in here somewhere.

We played together for hours every day, and I enjoyed my time with you — watching you grow and learn and explore. Hanging out with you was the best and brightest part of every day in my otherwise grey life.

And then, you began to individuate about the same time you found language. "No, I do dat!" or "I wan' dat!"

Vigilant in my commitment to "no limits," I tried to figure out how to help you feel empowered, to build your confidence in your abilities, and to get what you wanted in the most respectful and powerful way possible.

When I fed or dressed you, I gave you choices. You always felt so big after you made a decision for yourself. You still do, don't you?

Trying to keep you limitless and empowered around other people who were so fearful and/or negative was really difficult. Remember when you wanted to climb the big tree and Grandma freaked out? "Aaron, get down! You are going to fall down and break your head!" I nearly lost my mind on her. *Why would you even put that possibility in his head? Now it's a possibility!* I would do what I could to undo it by affirming who you really are and allowing you to do it anyway (and of course, asking Grandma to keep her fear to herself), "Honey, you can climb the tree. You're strong and have good balance. Just pay attention to where you're stepping and ask for help if you start to feel worried."

"*Big Man, use your words. What do you want?*"

When you wanted something and were using those sweet little manipulation tactics (crying, tantrums, etc.), I would wait for you to take a breath and say, "Big Man, use your words. What do you want? I can't understand you when you're screaming and crying." You would eventually calm yourself down and find some words to ask for what you wanted or to express whatever emotion had initiated the fit.

And then it started to happen. You started to use my tactics against me. Oh yeah — you remember, don't you? Wait! You still do that to me! LOL!

"Mommy?" You could tell I was upset as I was preparing your lunch. I flung the bread onto the plate, slapped the peanut butter and jelly on it, threw it together, and slammed the fridge after adding some veggies.

"Yes, Honey?" I tried to be calm and sweet for you. After all, it wasn't *your* fault that I was angry.

When you knew you had my attention, you finished, "Mommy, use your words."

Oh my goodness! I laughed out loud, seeing that you were clearly using my stuff against me...or *for* me.

"Big Man, you are *so* smart. You're right. I need to call her back and tell her that I didn't like the way she was talking to me. I deserve respect and kindness. Right?"

"Right!" I'm sure that at two years old, you had no idea what all that meant, but your emphatic agreement was cute and helpful nonetheless.

And then there was the time when I saw you holding your tears in and said, "Buddy, it's okay to cry," to which you quickly responded, "But you always go to your room to cry."

Caught me there!

And then there was that horrible day in the parking lot. That wasn't about *you* at all. I wasn't really angry with you — *I was angry with me.* You were just a sweet, tired little boy who wanted a

And then there was that horrible day in the parking lot. That wasn't about you at all...I was angry with me.

new stuffed animal, but the desperation in your exhausted tears mirrored the desperation I was feeling in every other area of my life, and I lost control when it all hit me at once.

The fact that I couldn't afford the item mirrored my shame and fear around money. *How am I unable to pay for a $5 stuffed animal?!? How are we ever going to make it?*

The fact that you were crying and I couldn't make it better mirrored how I was feeling in most of my relationships. *Everyone is mad at or disappointed in me, and it doesn't matter how hard I try, I can't make any of them happy.*

The fact that this all happened in front of people and I felt myself losing control mirrored my dread of what was coming. *I feel like a powerless fraud that is about to be found out.*

I dragged you out of that store and spanked you because that's what I was doing mentally and emotionally *to myself*. I was trying to punish myself into a new reality.

And you, My Sweet Boy, got caught in the crossfire of the internal war that was going on long before you were even conceived.

What if every time he irritates, frustrates, or challenges me, he's just mirroring back something I need to work on or heal?

Your growth process was easy, unlimited, and crazy energetic (like all of those crazy fast and hungry caterpillars!), and it was a painful mirror at times — providing such a contrast to my own slow, limited, painful process. That is, until I started to see that my reactions to you could help me see where I was limited…and your natural growth process could be a model for *me* in the middle of that reaction. My own growth process (healing and transformation) accelerated when I started to see this.

What if every time he irritates or challenges me, he's just mirroring back something I need to work on or heal?

Two Little Caterpillars

"Aaron, you broke my mirror! I told you to get out of here. You're a bad boy!" The venomous rage pierced my ears and my blood hit a hard boil.

How dare she talk to him like that! He's not bad! He's curious! I had turned off the kitchen sink and sprinted toward the bathroom where the exchange was happening, ready to knock her out for calling you "bad." These mommy feelings can get crazy sometimes. I'm just sayin'…

No, really. I *was* ready to shake her and trying to figure out how I should handle the situation when, about half-way there, I heard your sweet and unusually stern little voice, "Grandma, I am *not* a bad boy! I made a bad choice…I'm sorry I broke your mirror."

I stopped in my tracks. *Oh my goodness! Now he's using my stuff against others!*

I saw your little almost three-year-old frame in the doorway, staring straight into her eyes, and waited for her response. *Seriously. What can she say to that?*

"Oh, you're right. You're not bad. Okay…" Caught completely off-guard, all she wanted to do was get you out of her space. (You know you're a mirror for everyone in your life, not just me, right?) "Get out of here so you don't cut your feet on the glass. I'll clean it up."

When you turned around, all I could do was smile and nod to affirm that you had handled that like a champ before I turned and walked back to the kitchen.

As I finished the dishes, I shook my head in disbelief. *He just successfully detached his worth from his behavior. He gets it! He knows that he is innately good, and that nothing he does can change that. It's all just choices — good ones or bad ones. And he took responsibility…at three! Is my work done, or what? I think we just broke a legacy here.*

Now all I have to do is figure out how to detach my worth from my behavior. When did that start for me?

I watched you stop and take a deep breath, as if your soul was digesting what had just happened, and I wondered what was going on inside of that head of yours.

What if we are supposed to work together to break legacies of limitation?

More than Words

"Mommy, I had a bad dream." You had found your way to the side of my bed and tapped on my arm to wake me up. I reached out to pull you into bed next to me.

"Do you want to tell me about it?" Your whimper broke my heart, but not as much as your next words would.

"We were all dying, and we couldn't find the *real* you…" I took a deep breath, afraid of where this was going, and waited. "You were gone and you didn't tell us…"

"Awww…I'm sorry, Big Man. Well, I'm right here. You wanna stay in here and snuggle for a little bit?"

"Uh-huh…" You rubbed the tears away as you drifted quickly back to sleep in my arms.

The real me is missing, and he knows it. I've reinforced every powerful message I can imagine, and it's working, and yet somehow he knows that he is only experiencing a shadow of the real me. What will happen to him if I don't find the real me? Will he grow up to feel like this has all been a lie — something I wanted for him but wasn't possible for me or anyone else?

I stroked your hair as the tears rolled down my face.

> *The real me is missing, and he knows it.*

Big Man, I promise I'm going to find the real me and bring her back to you and your daddy. You deserve more than words. You deserve a real-life model of the happiness, love, and possibility I've promised is here for you. I don't want you to grow up, modeling a shadow.

I knew I had a lot of work to do, and I silently prayed that this community and training I was stepping into with Lisa would show me how to do it.

3
Upside-Down Danger

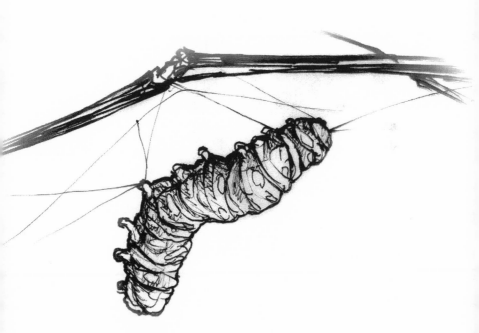

"Challenges are gifts that force us
to search for a new center of gravity.
Don't fight them.
Just find a new way to stand."

Oprah Winfrey

"Mommy, where'd they go?" The concern in your voice made my heart sink.

"They're not in the container?" I asked, as I moved toward you and the jar.

"Oh, there they are!" You pointed so I could see.

"Where?" I asked, tipping my head to look up and under the lid.

"They are all done eating?" you asked.

"It sure looks like it. Gee, they are even bigger than last night! Looks like they are not interested in the food anymore. And look how *slow* they're moving."

"They are full."

The matter-of-fact tone of your voice made me laugh. "Yep, big tummies. I am going to get your breakfast while you watch them."

I was scrambling your eggs when I heard you shout, "Uh-oh!"

"What?"

"Look!" You motioned me over with big concern on your face. "He's falling off the top. Help him." Peeking into the container, I saw that one of the caterpillars had just gone upside-down.

"Oh my goodness. No, he's not falling. This is part of the process. He has to be upside-down before he can create his cocoon."

"Cocoon?"

"Yes, they build a safe little place for themselves where they change from a caterpillar to a butterfly."

"Oh…" Your eyes got even bigger, trying to figure this whole process out.

I sat down next to you while you ate your eggs and watched the caterpillars with anticipation. One had gone upside-down, but there were three more.

I want to see it happen.

I want to see it happen.

It wasn't long before the next one dropped down. I was startled at how quickly it went from clutching the top of the container to hanging upside-down from the cloth at the top of the jar.

"Wow. Looks like when they're ready, they're ready!"

We finished our meal, and then you reached for the jar to take it with us into the backyard.

"Hey, Buddy. We need to be *really* careful with them now. See that tiny little string? That's all that's holding them on that cloth. If we move the jar too fast or without care, we could knock one off and mess up their process."

"Okay, Mommy. I will be careful." You pulled your hands back, your eyes full of wonder and glued to the jar, awaiting the next phase of transformation.

Caterpillar Upset

"Mommy, I don't want…" you whined for the fourth time in thirty minutes as you rubbed the tears out of your eyes and plopped down on the floor.

It was very unusual to see you so upset, and just like any other parent, I wanted to make it better somehow — to find something to soothe the upset — but all of my suggestions (hunger? thirst? tiredness? etc.) had been met with, "I don't want…"

Aaron, what is going on? I noticed the frustration building in me and took a deep breath. *I've got phone calls starting in a few minutes, and I've got to get your breakfast done. What is up with you today?*

"Mommy…" It was a plea for focused attention.

I guess our breakfast and my phone calls will have to wait.

"Big Man, what's the matter?" I turned the stove off and sat down on the floor next to you, hoping you would find the words.

"I don't know…" you whimpered.

You looked extremely tired, almost listless, and I felt your head for fever.

No, no fever.

"Does your body feel bad anywhere?"

"No, my body is okay."

"Are you sad? mad? confused?" I said, pausing between each word until you responded with a shake of your head.

"Hmmm…maybe today is just one of those days that happen sometimes, when something isn't quite right, but we can't put a finger on it."

I held my arms out to offer a hug. Looking relieved that the questions had stopped, you crawled over to me, sat on my lap, and put your head on my shoulder.

I wrapped my arms around your three-year-old frame and snuggled you for a long time there on the floor, trying to tune into whatever was going on in your heart and mind. I couldn't tell. It wasn't quite sadness or confusion, and it definitely wasn't anger. It just felt "off."

I held my arms out to offer a hug. Looking relieved that the questions had stopped, you crawled over to me... and put your head on my shoulder.

As I held you close, I felt incredibly grateful for the insight of the child development specialist who'd crossed our path years before and seriously shaped my approach to moments like these.

"It looks like he's doing really great. Isn't it fun to watch him grow and learn?"

"Yes. I'm really enjoying it." I smiled, watching you match the shaped block to the same shaped hole in the ball toy.

"Yes, it's fun, and... Well, there's one thing that I always share with new mommies because no one else seems to." She smiled, leaning toward me as if to communicate the importance of what she was about to share, and continued, "When children learn something new — like how to crawl, walk, or string words together, or anything really — that big achievement is usually followed by some regression."

"What do you mean?" Now I leaned forward, feeling the significance of what she was trying to tell me.

> *She finished, "When this happens, don't be concerned, and don't try to force him...Just let him be. It's a natural process..."*

"Well, they may learn how to string words together and do it for a few days, and then wake up one morning and struggle to find words at all, let alone string them together in a sentence that makes sense." I nodded to show her I understood, and she finished, "When this happens, *don't be concerned*, and *don't try to force him* to do anything. *Just let him be.* It's a natural process during which the rest of the child — mentally and emotionally — catches up with their growth and new reality."

Well, that's interesting. I never heard this in all my years of education, but it makes sense with what I know about the brain and the subconscious and how they work together to solve problems and master skills. I don't know how many times I've encouraged people to stop pushing and working so hard to solve a problem or master a skill — to just let go and let the natural processes inside of them do it for them. Hmmmm…

Over the next year, I watched this happen without fail. You'd achieve something, and then you'd forget for a few days; and sometimes, you wouldn't regress in the area you had grown in, but you'd get *really* emotional. For instance, when you started to string words together, you didn't regress with the language, you just got really irritable.

This must be one of those days. He did some good work with numbers yesterday, I thought as I held you and let the phone ring through to voicemail. *He must be catching up — recalibrating to his new level of understanding.*

I pulled you closer and felt your body relax into me. *I am gonna have to be extra careful with you today — not allow myself to get too frustrated and make a big deal of it. Maybe we can have a down-day today — just snuggle and play in the garden.*

After we watched the entire butterfly metamorphosis, I started to call these days "upside-down days" because that's what it feels like, right? Somehow, something has changed, and you don't see things (yourself, people, circumstances, etc.) the way you did before. It can feel like everything has turned upside-down. And if you don't know what's happening, it can be very confusing and upsetting, even scary.

Caterpillar Upside-Down

When I started the training program with Lisa and her two master facilitators, I was so excited. Not only had I just reconnected with the power of my magic egg (the value I had to give to the world through my message *and* the God-given ability I had to ask, believe, and receive a *Secret* Teacher into my life), but I'd always been at the top of my class through school. So when I saw that there was a written curriculum to memorize and a clear process to follow, I figured it would be pretty easy, and I'd be one of the first to get certified.

Why wouldn't this be like everything else I've set out to do?

But it wasn't. Not even close. I couldn't memorize the curriculum. I couldn't connect with the teens. I couldn't share my story powerfully. And, at the end of the year-long program, a bunch of my friends got certified and I didn't!

What is wrong with me? Why can't I memorize the curriculum? I used to memorize so quickly and easily? Why can't I nail my presentations the way I used to?

It had happened…

This little caterpillar had officially gone upside-down.

And boy, was I angry!

Why can't I get it together? I have to study more. I have to go to more workshops to watch it in real-time. I have to…

Upside-Down Danger

"Ummm…am I about to get in trouble?" You had paused mid-sentence to ask the question.

"No, Honey. Why do you ask?"

"Well, you're giving me that look."

I smiled at your fearlessness and calmly replied, "What look?"

"The 'I'm getting upset' look. I just thought maybe it was something I was saying?"

"No, Sweetie. But thank you for paying such close attention to how I'm feeling. It's not about you or what you are saying, but I *am* feeling a little upside-down today."

"How come?" Such sweet curiosity.

"Well, ummmm…I'm pretty frustrated, actually. I've always been *really good* at school and learning new skills and memorizing, but I can't seem to do it for Lisa's program. I don't understand, cuz I'm using all the same strategies I used before, and nothing is working. It's like my whole world has turned upside-down, and I can't quite understand what I am looking at yet. Do you ever feel that way at school — frustrated because you are learning something new, and it doesn't quite make sense yet? You *know* you're going to get it, but sometimes you *feel* like you're never going to?"

"Yes, I felt like that with subtraction last week. Yuck!" Your affirmative nod was so comforting.

"Well, that's exactly how I'm feeling — totally upside-down. And sometimes, my 'upside-down' looks like crankiness, sadness, impatience, anger, or even confusion. Actually, I have felt all of that in this program." I looked up, surprised at how attentive you still were, at just five years old.

"I've even been acting strange in the trainings. I have been talking *way* more than usual, almost like I'm trying to show-off, when the truth is that I feel like I don't know what I'm doing. Isn't that crazy?" I didn't wait for you to confirm that I was crazy. "You know how sometimes, you do things without thinking about it, and it appears to bug other people?"

"Oh yeah. Like when I'm bouncing in the house, and Grandma gets on my case."

"Exactly, well, I don't know if you know this, but you usually 'act up' like that right after you learn something new. It's like you just realized that

It's almost like there is a fight between the Old Big You and the New Bigger You.

you're bigger, but you're not sure what being bigger means yet, so you bounce, you push your limits with us to see how far your new power goes, and you get cranky. It's almost like there is a fight between the Old Big You and the New Bigger You. The Old Big You wants you to stay the same as you were because it feels safer and easier than trying to figure out how to be New Bigger You, cuz you've never been that before, right? "

"Yeah, but I don't like it when I'm bouncing and I get yelled at. Sometimes, she doesn't even yell; she just looks at me mean, and I feel bad."

"Yeah, I know. Do you know that she does that because she doesn't know *why* you're bouncing? All she can think is that what you are doing is driving her crazy, that you are interrupting what she is doing, that you might break something, and that she wants you to stop. Our upside-down feelings and actions definitely affect the people around us; it's actually kinda dangerous if we and the people around us don't know what's going on. But that doesn't mean it's okay for them to yell at us."

"Yeah, but I still don't like getting yelled at or looked at mean."

"Yeah, me neither. It definitely doesn't help us get through the upside-down any faster." As soon as I said it, I saw what my real problem had been.

Oh my goodness. This is what I've been doing to myself in this program! I have worn myself out. I've been pushing and pushing — more workshops, more phone calls, more volunteering. But what else can I do?

Shedding the Fuzzies

"If you really knew me, you'd know that I…" The words cut my throat on their way out, but I was done pretending. Pretending had not gotten me anywhere, and I was determined to tell the truth and deal with it, no matter how hard it was.

Two years after I had started the program, I was sitting knee to knee with a perfect stranger, just like I'd done in dozens of workshops, but this time, I was telling them my deepest, darkest, most shameful secrets.

"You'd know that my smile is plastic… You'd know that I always excel in my work, but it's never good enough for me…You'd know that everyone thinks I'm 'bound for greatness,' but I feel like a broken fraud…" I took a deep breath and continued, comforted by the kind eyes looking back at me.

I was sitting knee to knee with a perfect stranger, telling them my deepest, darkest, most shameful secrets.

"You'd know that I'm dead broke and suffocating with debt… You'd know that I am scared that we are going to be poor forever…" Another deep breath followed by slow tears. I could feel the desperation bubbling as I shed the masks that had been keeping me safe.

Safe…and miserable…and dying inside…

"You'd know that I use food to make myself feel better… You'd know that I am scared that I can't fix my marriage… You'd know that I lost my mind and hurt my child…"

When her eyes brimmed with tears, the dam in me broke. Shaking and sobbing, I pulled my knees up to my chest and turned my body in my chair, as if to protect myself from the judgment I expected. I felt naked and ashamed and scared.

What did I just do? I just told someone how completely messed up I am! The tears continued, now driven largely by fear of consequences. Was she going to tell them how messed up I was? *They are going to kick me out of the program. Well, maybe they should. How can I help anyone else when I am like this? This is my reality right now!*

But instead of judging me, she knelt by my chair, wrapped both arms around my shaking body, and cried with me.

On my way home that evening, while struggling to see the road through my swollen eyes, I thought about that woman rocking me back and forth like I was a little child, consoling me with her embrace. *How is that possible? I just showed her all of my uglies, and she showed me nothing but love. No judgment. No advice. Nothing but love.*

"Amanda, do you remember?" The still, small voice spoke through the silence as a memory flashed through my mind.

But instead of judging me, she knelt by my chair, wrapped both arms around my shaking body, and cried with me.

When your Aunt Lyssie was a little baby, I was rocking her to sleep in the kitchen when I was given a vision. I was watching a slightly older version of her run on the playground when I noticed a log just barely protruding out of the sand. I screamed across the playground to warn her that she was about to trip, but in all of her excitement about getting to the slide, she didn't see it and totally wiped out. Even before she hit the ground, I was running toward her. When she looked up at me, her face was a mess of blood and muddy tears.

I pulled her into my arms and started to rock her back and forth to console her.

"Amanda, would you be angry with her?"

"What? For not seeing? For falling? No way." I was almost angry with Him for asking such a ridiculous question.

"Right. So why would you expect me to be angry with you when you make a mistake? You are my beloved child, and I am far more concerned about getting you bandaged up than punishing you for not knowing what you don't know."

"Yes, I remember," I whispered quietly in response to the voice.

"Don't be so hard on yourself. You didn't see the logs. You've got some scrapes and wounds, and it's okay. It can all be healed…if you let yourself feel the upside-down and be in the process. It's not going to work if you beat yourself up through it."

Didn't I tell Aaron the same thing a few weeks ago? What if I stopped fighting it and just went with it — like Aaron does?

I was upside-down, and I had to just relax into it like the caterpillar does — like you did that day when "I don't know…" was all you could say but enough for me to know that you were in a natural process and we could both relax into it.

And in a split second, I saw myself cradled in Divine Arms.

"Let me hold and rock you through the process. Let me show you how to create a safe, sacred space around you — a cocoon — to heal and transform."

And, of course, He used my experience with you to show me.

4

Committed Cocoon

"The first step to change...
is accepting your reality right now.
Honoring your process. Compassionate
self-awareness leads to change; harsh self-
criticism only holds the pattern in place...
Be gentle with yourself as you would with a
child. Be gentle but firm. Give yourself the
space to grow. But remember that the
timing is in God's hands, not yours."

Dan Millman

"Mommy, say nigh-night to the caterpillars." You walked over to the jar on the game table and looked in. We had decided to move it away from all of the activity in the kitchen to keep them safe.

"Good night, caterpillars. Happy dreams." I waited for you at the bottom of the stairs.

"What happened? Where did they go?" You searched the jar for them, and I came over to help you.

"Wow, they already made their cocoons, Aaron. The caterpillars are in those little things hanging from the top of the jar. See that one in the middle? His cocoon isn't done yet. His butt is still poking out at the top a little. See it?"

You laughed and pressed your nose even harder against the side of the jar to see in.

"Oh...they're ready for nigh-night, too?"

"Yep, it's bedtime, but I think *they* are going to sleep for a few days. In the morning, we can attach the cloth they are hanging from to the inside of the bungalow, so they can sleep in there as long as they need to."

"Okay, Mommy." You rubbed your eyes and yawned, obviously ready to leave the cocoons until the next morning.

"Come on, Sweetie. It's time for you to have happy dreams about caterpillars and butterflies."

The next morning, you were ready to help me move them. Your eyes were full of wonder as you watched me unfold the big, netted tent-like bungalow.

"Sweetie, this is something Mommy needs to do. If you move too fast, the cocoon could fall off."

"Mommy, it's big enough for me to go in there?" You almost screeched the question in your excitement.

"Yes, look, here's the door."

"Ooooh! Can I go in there and help you?"

"Sweetie, this is something Mommy needs to do. If you do it, and you move too fast or accidentally hit one of them, the cocoon could fall off and then the caterpillar won't be able to finish becoming a butterfly."

I opened the jar and very carefully removed the cloth with the hanging cocoons. For a moment, I forgot that you were three years old. You showed such incredible restraint while you watched me. It was obvious that you wanted to help, but it was as if you somehow knew that you were witnessing a sacred process and wanted to make sure the caterpillars were going to be okay.

"Why don't you get some flowers and leaves from the garden. Then, when they wake up and come out of their cocoons, they will have something to eat."

You left to get some flowers, while I gingerly finished attaching the cloth to the top of the bungalow with a safety pin. *There! We did it. And none of them fell.*

I watched you spread the flowers around the bottom of the bungalow and tried to help you understand that it would be a while. "Buddy, they might be in there for days — or even a week or more. They have a lot of work they are doing in there — growing long legs and wings and dreaming about flying."

"Okay, Mommy. Happy dreams, caterpillars."

For the next few days, we checked the bungalow for any sign of movement in the morning when we woke up, after lunch, and then right before bed.

A few days into the process, I could see you were getting impatient and dangerously close to the bungalow.

"Sweetie, be very careful around the bungalow. If you hit it, one of those cocoons could come loose and fall down.

We don't want to hurt them."

"Okay, Mommy." You walked away, determined to wait.

Later that day, I heard your little voice, "No! Grandma! Don't touch it! You'll hurt them! They're not ready!"

"I just want to look, Aaron."

You fell to your knees, sobbing, "I'm sorry, little butterfly."

"No, Grandma! You made him fall! Now he can't be a butterfly!" I walked into the room in time to see your face scrunch up with pain. Refusing to listen to your warning, she had accidentally hit the corner of the bungalow, and just like I had told you would happen, one of the cocoons detached and plummeted toward the floor of the bungalow.

Your face turned bright red, and you fell on your knees, sobbing, "I'm sorry, little butterfly."

Grandma apologized and quickly left the room, not knowing what to do.

I cradled you in my arms and rocked you back and forth, trying to comfort you, but you were inconsolable.

"Mommy, I…told…her," you stammered through your tears.

"I know, Sweetie. It was an accident. Maybe he can still finish his process on the ground. Let's hope together that he will be okay."

"When the cocoon hit the ground," My heart broke with yours. Not only was I heartbroken to feel your grief in the sobs shaking your body, but I also was sad for the caterpillar that might never become a butterfly, or worse, become a butterfly that could not take flight.

Look at how easy it is to mess up such a divinely beautiful process.

I glanced toward the bungalow. *Look at how easy it is to mess up such a divinely beautiful process.*

Of course, I flashed on that horrible moment in the parking lot — when I was sure that I had done irreparable damage — and silently prayed that your growth process would not be limited because of my behavior that day.

I've done everything I know how to create a safe space for you to grow and become — taken such great care with my words and actions — all I can do is pray that the wound will heal as I learn how to show you unconditional love.

I don't know how many times you checked the bungalow that day, but my heart broke every time you walked over to it. I suspected that if I were close enough, I would hear you apologizing to the little guy on the floor again and quietly hoping that he would be okay.

You were so committed to keeping those cocoons safe after that, and so was I…

They didn't happen often, but when they did, you went all the way with them, and this tantrum was no different.

It was one of those mornings. You'd woken up feeling upside-down, and we'd spent some time snuggling and reading a book, and then in the garden chasing butterflies, trying to relax into the upside-down a bit. I'd discovered that sometimes, it just took a little bit of distraction — redirecting your energy toward more pleasant-feeling activities and taking your mind off how you were feeling — to help you move through the process more quickly.

And it had worked for a while that morning, until you'd asked, in your sweet three-year-old voice, to watch your favorite movie *Finding Nemo*, and I'd said, "No, Sweetie.

We don't have enough time before we have to leave for our appointment. But we can watch it as soon as…"

Before I'd finished the sentence, you'd thrown yourself on the floor and begun screaming at the top of your lungs, "No! No! No! I don't want to go! I want to watch Nemo!"

Startled by the sudden outburst, I felt my heart start to race and my own anger surface. *Why does this have to be so freaking hard? I just need this to be easy. I don't have the energy to fight with him! I don't want to fight with him. Actually, I'd like to get on the ground and pound the floor too. Wow. He is triggering my stuff today!*

Committed to not letting my temper be part of my parenting again, I took a deep breath and stopped packing the toy bag, sat on the floor about five feet away from you, and asked myself, *What does your child need from you right now?*

What does your child need from you right now?

Stuck in my own fatigue and frustration, the answer didn't easily emerge, so I navigated my way out by putting myself "in your shoes." *What do I need when I am this angry?*

Sometimes, I just need to pound the floor. I don't really want to interrupt that. It's probably good for him, like the punching bag is good for me. He's not hurting anyone. And I'm not going to be able to reason with him in this state.

So, I waited patiently for you to finish, and thought about how important this whole "expressing your feelings" business was.

When did I stop feeling like it was okay to express my emotions, and why?

When did I stop feeling like it was okay to express my emotions, and why? Was it because whenever I shared hurt, anger, or sadness with someone, it seemed to make them feel bad too? Was it because when I had been hurt, they would get angry on my behalf? Or that when I was angry, they often became angry too? I didn't want anyone to feel how I was feeling.

As I watched you scream and pound, I thought back to some of the messages that were communicated by the adults in my life early on and how they had been received so differently than intended. "If you don't have anything nice to say, don't say anything at all." "If you say that, it might upset them." Or "Use your words to uplift and encourage."

And no matter what I was feeling, the adults always tried to help me feel better — different than I was feeling — which somehow made me think that those feelings were bad, and that I needed to stay away from them...or at least not tell anyone I was feeling them.

I'm sure none of the kind adults in my life meant to communicate that it wasn't okay to have or express my feelings. They were probably just repeating what they'd heard the adults in their lives say, not understanding the potential impact of them.

It actually didn't take very long for you to notice that I wasn't reacting to your fit. After just a few minutes, you were sitting up and pulling yourself together. "Mommy, I want to watch Nemo."

"Aaron, it sounds like you are very angry, and I understand. I don't like it when I want something fast, and I can't get it right away either."

"Yeah, I don't like it." Your lower lip was in full-pout.

"I can see that." I had to hide my smile. You're pretty cute when you pout, even now. But you know that, don't you?

I took another deep breath. *What does your child need from you right now?*

What do I need when I am feeling this powerless to get what I want? The tears and anger are coming because he feels powerless to change anything, right? What if there's a way for him to get what he wants? Wouldn't that empower him?

"Big Man, we have a problem we need to solve together, and you are a really smart guy, so I think we can figure something out together. You want to watch your movie, and I have to make sure we don't miss our appointment. What can we do?"

"Can I watch some of the movie now, and then watch the end when we get home?"

"Great idea! Why didn't I think of that? We have forty-five minutes until we have to leave, which is only enough time to watch half the movie."

"Okay."

Seriously, why didn't I think of this? Oh yeah, because I didn't want him to throw a tantrum when I turned the movie off.

"Okay, but if we do it this way, then we have to agree that when it's time to go, you will pause it and come with

Mommy. No fussing, okay? Because you are agreeing?"

"Okay, Mommy." You smiled as you got up, planted a kiss on my cheek, and ran to the living room to turn on your movie.

Forty-five minutes later, I walked into the living room and asked you to turn off the movie. "Mommy, just five more minutes?" You asked it with a smile that told me you knew you were just testing me.

Ahhh…yes…he's gotta see how far that power goes, doesn't he?

"No, Sweetie. This was our agreement." I smiled back.

"Okay!" you said, as you turned it off and jumped out of the chair.

He actually looks happy that I said 'no.' I wonder what that's about? Maybe it's just being able to trust my word?

My Very Own Cocoon

"Amanda, it's okay. Take a deep breath." She could see the battle waging behind my eyes.

Why can't you get this dang lesson? You know this. It's the easiest one!

But I knew why I couldn't, and I took a deep breath as I relented to the truth of it. *I'm unable to facilitate it because I don't believe any of it.*

I looked up, with tears welling.

"Amanda, you know why you had trouble with this lesson?"

"Yes, it's because I don't believe any of my Powerful Self-Talk." I looked down at the ground, shame flushing my face. *After two years, I still haven't done this.*

"That's right. And do you know it's okay?"

"*All you have to do is learn to love yourself through this process... We're not going anywhere.*"

Surprised, I lifted my eyes and shook my head. *No, it's not okay. How can she say it's okay?!?*

"Amanda, you are doing the work. You are in the process. You have been working your tail off, and we all see it." She paused and waited for me to breathe again. "When you got to us, you were drowning, Baby Girl. We saw it. It looked like you were using up your last bit of oxygen. And now, you're here, and you're breathing again. You've been doing the work, and you've got a little more color and light…and there's still more work to do. All you have to do is learn how to love yourself through this process. And it's okay. We're not going anywhere." She held her arms out to offer a hug, and of course, I fell apart.

You're not going anywhere? It doesn't matter how much I act up, drive your facilitators crazy with questions and attitude, and take forever to get through this dang program? You will still be here?

I sat back down after a good, long cry on her shoulder. I had never experienced that type of committed safe space before. I felt like a bull in a china cabinet, inside of a cocoon, making all kinds of discomfort and mess with all of my honesty and anger.

But they all stayed. The facilitators and colleagues all stayed side-by-side on my journey, cheering me on (like you were at home), witnessing the transformation inside of the cocoon…until one day, it happened. I figured out what I had been missing in this program.

Committed Cocoon Transformation

"My negative self-talk has caused me to push everyone that I love away…"

I took a deep breath as the tears began to fall and ignored the impulse to pull my knees up to my chest or run out of the workshop full of teens.

They have no idea. I'm here for me as much as I am here for them.

I thought about the last workshop, when I had shared transparently and wondered if the lady was going to rat me out, and been shocked when she had just cried with me.

"My negative self-talk has caused me to feel alone, unheard, and misunderstood…to lie about how I'm feeling…to feel unsafe, defensive, and angry."

As the words flew out of my mouth, my eyes widened in tearful surprise. Up to this point, I had been able to express sad and angry, but I had never said the word "unsafe" before.

That's it. I don't feel safe anywhere, except with Aaron. He's the only one able to give me unconditional love right now. And even if the others were to try, I feel too fragile to witness the impact my transparency would have on them. I don't want them to feel bad. I just want them to know…me…and love me anyway.

"My negative self-talk has caused me to hurt my body with sugar and caffeine and crazy diets…to give myself dirty looks when I pass the mirror…to say cruel things to myself…things that I wouldn't even say to enemies…"

Holy crap! The light bulb clicked on. *How can I ask anyone else for a safe space when I am not giving it to myself? Of course I'm afraid of what they're going to say…I'm already beating myself to a pulp!*

The light bulb clicked on. How can I ask anyone else for a safe space when I am not giving it to myself?

Just then, the exercise shifted.

"My powerful self-talk tells me that I am worthy of a safe space, of unconditional love and support…that I have to learn how to give these to myself before I can ask anyone else to do it for me…that I can figure out how to do this…"

How am I going to give myself a safe space?

I thought about you and that Nemo episode, how upset you had been and how I had tried to make it safe for you to feel that way, to find your power in the situation, to work together to solve the problem, to make agreements for both of us to stay safe.

I looked up and realized that the model of a safe space given to me in this training program was basically the same model I had just "made up" with you that day on the floor.

Has He been trying to show me this process through Aaron for years?

And how did I do that? Oh yeah…by asking myself what I needed when I felt that way. So I had the answer this whole time, and yet it never occurred to me to give it to myself before asking others to give it to me? Is this what God meant when he said, 'Let me show you how to create a safe, sacred space around you — a cocoon — to heal and transform'? Has He been trying to show me this process through Aaron for years, and I just didn't get it?

The tears rolled down my face as I realized again that I had been at the center of a divine intervention. And you, of course, were one of my angels in this process.

Thank you…

The realization that I needed to give myself a safe space shifted everything...fast. Giving myself this type of unconditional love and safety allowed me to tell my whole truth, to take better care of myself emotionally and physically, and to be more powerful inside of this type of work. Every time pain, anger, or shame came up, I would ask myself, *How can I love myself through this?* I made that commitment to myself and acted on it by giving myself time to journal, take a bath, or call a friend to really feel the feelings and heal myself inside of my new safe space.

In hardly any time at all, I had done enough work — not all of it, but enough — to become a certified facilitator and help others through the transformational process as well. Thrilled and grateful, I got ready to close some big contracts to facilitate teen transformation as a vendor for major government entities and schools.

Life had finally changed for the better, and then, it all fell apart again...

The Death of the Caterpillar

My three years of transformation and marketing the transformational workshops to my community had paid off. I had big contracts ready to be signed with the county and school districts, the decision-makers were excited to bring the program to their kids, and I was on my way to changing lives and making good money.

This is it. This is finally happening. I am finally doing what I am meant to do!

But almost as soon as I completed my certification, the market crashed. The people who had been fighting to bring the program into their communities stopped answering my phone calls, and my dream crumbled.

I looked around the ballroom full of excited entrepreneurs at Ursula's first big event and immediately felt alone and angry.

I am sick and tired of this happening to me! It's not fair. The doors slammed on my dreams of becoming a teacher, a writing instructor, an editor, and now a facilitator! Why? What is wrong with me?

"What about True to Intention?" The still, small voice intruded over the activity in the room.

What about it? I responded sarcastically. A few months before the market crashed, I'd been inspired to change the name of my editing business (what had been barely paying our bills during the training program) to True to Intention. It resonated with me, capturing the message that had led me to Lisa — the one that had been developed through our Butterfly Bungalow experience: We are born magic eggs, with everything we need to become what we are meant to become around us, but something happens, and we stop believing in those dreams that were placed within us. Our work is to remember our intention and be true to it.

"*What about True to Intention?" The still, small voice intruded over the activity in the room.*

When I'd said '*yes*' to my purpose, Lisa walked into a Sizzler behind me only three months later. In every teen workshop, transformation occurred when they realized they already have the power to change their lives. And the testimonials from my authors always went something like this: "Thank you for helping me stay true to my real message." True to Intention felt so right to me. I had to move forward, yet something was holding me back.

"You know, Amanda…" It was the last break of the day, and I'd mentioned my dream again to a few friends. "I think you should ask yourself why you're all talk. It's a great idea. Where are the business cards?" Her voice was full of love, but razor sharp, and it cut through me.

Silently, I turned on my heel and tore out of the building, racing to get to my car before the dam broke, trying to ignore the voices that started shouting, *"You're never going to get yourself together."* I stumbled across the parking lot and struggled to steady my hand to unlock the door. *"You're such a disappointment."* I sobbed all the way home. *"Your family will starve because everything you do falls apart."*

> *Burying my wet face, I screamed at God, Why is this happening again?*

I got in my pajamas, turned off all the lights, and collapsed into bed. *"You're a fraud — wait 'til everyone finds out! They thought you were bound for greatness, and look!"* The venom burned my ears and seared through my heart. Desperate, I covered my head to shut the voices out.

Burying my wet face in my pillow, I screamed at God. *Why is this happening again? Why would you give me a message, put the people in my life to make it happen, and then take it all away again? Of course I don't want to move forward with my dream because the others were taken away! Every single one of them — teaching, online instructing, editing, and now this! And as far as I can tell, it's your fault! You opened the doors, and then you let them slam! Where have you been?*

What am I doing in this life?...Oh no! I am a fraud! Here I was ready to be certified to teach teens how to fall in love with themselves, and I was asking myself if I should keep living? The room swirled, and the pressure in my chest grew.

"You don't deserve to live."

Pull it together, Amanda. You have a husband, a little boy, and a family to live for. You can't leave them behind. Pull yourself together! As soon as I asked myself the question How?, I remembered a tool we taught the teens. I reached for my journal and, cocooning myself into a safe space, I started writing. "My negative self-talk tells me that I'm worthless, that nothing will ever change, that I'm a disappointment, that I should just give up. It tells me that I'm a fraud, that my broken dreams are my fault, that I'm not good enough to have them…"

I trembled as years of pain coursed through my veins, out through the pen, and onto the tear-smeared paper. I took a deep breath, silencing my resistance to doing what I knew

I had to do next, and started to write. "My powerful self-talk tells me that I have a beautiful family to live for, that I have purpose, and am worthy of my dreams. It tells me that I am a good mother and wife, that I am an incredible teacher who inspires, that I have a message and tools to help others. It reminds me that I have manifested miracles, that I have already made a difference, and that I have always been taken care of."

The venomous voices silenced, I heard the still, small voice, "Amanda, do you see? All of those broken dreams you have taken on as failures? They weren't failures. You're using your teaching skills every day (just not the way you expected), you're inspiring others to be better versions of themselves through your work (just not the way you expected), and you're living your message in your parenting, marriage, and career (just not the way you expected), and now you're going to use the transformational training you've just completed (just not the way you expected).

> "I never abandoned you. You just didn't recognize me. I WAS and AM all of the closed doors."

"The dreams didn't end because you weren't good enough or did something wrong. They ended because you got what you needed from them, and you needed to move to the next thing so you could do the work I have for you. I never abandoned you. You just didn't recognize me. *I WAS and AM all of the closed doors*, directing you to be True to *your* Intention and to help others be true to theirs. Beloved, dare to dream again. And lean into the discomfort. Relax into your upside-down like the caterpillar does. Love yourself through this. Trust that the transformation will happen...because it's meant to."

That was it. This caterpillar was officially no more. It had shed the last of its fuzzies, grown legs and wings, and was ready to break through the cocoon. But to do it, I had to let go of that safe space that had allowed me to do the work.

It was time. No one could do it for me, but you were right there to give me that final nudge and show me that.

5

Wing Training

"What lies behind us and what lies before us are tiny matters compared to what lies within us."

Ralph Waldo Emerson

"Mommy, it's moving!" I could hear your voice three rooms away and started running.

I don't want to miss it!

I got there just in time. The rustling that was happening inside the cocoon increased until we saw it — the opening at the bottom of the cocoon.

"Look! His legs!" Two legs and a head appeared, and it looked as if it was using both legs to push the cocoon completely open.

"Yeah, look at how hard he is working, Aaron. He is pushing that part away and wriggling his whole body trying to get out of there."

"Come on, butterfly! You can do it!" I smiled at your sweet cheer.

"Oh no, his wing." The concern in your voice made me take a closer look. "Is it broken?"

"It kinda looks like it. It's all crinkled. But I think that's just from being in the cocoon. Let's keep watching."

You continued cheering, and I couldn't help but join in. "Come on, butterfly! Stretch out those wings!"

Fully emerged, the butterfly began pumping his crinkly wings up and down, up and down. With every pump, the wings seemed to straighten out a bit.

And then another cocoon began to move, and we cheered all over again. All three hanging cocoons had broken open before you remembered the one on the ground.

A little tear streamed down your face as we watched him flail all over the bottom of the bungalow.

"Mommy, look. It's moving. Maybe he's okay."

We both held our breath while we watched him work his way out of the cocoon.

"Oh no, Mommy, look at his wing. It's broken."

"Awwww…Honey, I'm sorry."

"He can't fly?"

"I don't think so." A little tear streamed down your face as we watched him flail all over the bottom of the bungalow. Trying to pump his wings the way the others had, he was destroying what was left of his wing against the floor.

Hoping to encourage you, I asked, "Do you want to take the bungalow outside and see if they will fly to a flower?"

"Okay." Your slumped shoulders and sad countenance said everything else.

I picked the bungalow up at the top and carried it gently to the back yard, with you on my heels, and then set it down next to some bright flowers.

"Mommy, can I go in there?"

"Sure, just be careful." I opened the door and held it up while you crawled in. When you sat up, you were careful not to sit on the broken butterfly still flailing at the bottom. I saw the sadness wash over your face again, and then you lifted your eyes up to the other butterflies. Suddenly, you sparkled with wonder and then a little concern.

"Mommy, they're not flying."

"No, Honey. Not yet. It looks like they are practicing though. Look at them flutter those wings. Maybe they are building strength in their wings, so that when they fly, they are strong enough."

Just as I finished saying that, one of the butterflies floated down to your arm.

"Oooooohhhh…it tickles!" The smile lit up your whole face.

You were so very still, as you watched the butterfly walk up and down your arm, flap its wings, and then take a small flight from your arm to your knee and then to your hand.

"He flew," you whispered, trying not to scare him.

"Yeah, look at that. I think he likes you, Buddy. He's looking straight at you."

Another big smile.

"Maybe he's saying, 'Thank you for taking care of me.' You did a really good job taking care of the eggs and caterpillars and cocoons, Aaron. You must be proud of yourself for doing such a great job." The pride and gratitude you felt oozed all over the bungalow, and I thought about all the times that I have felt that way about you — when I have seen you accomplish something and felt so proud to be part of your journey.

"Pretty soon, we'll have to let them go, Aaron, so they can fly around, eat, and lay more magic eggs."

"Okay, can I just play with them a little more?"

"Absolutely. Let's enjoy them while we can."

Breakthrough Pains

"Mommy!" The excitement in your voice snapped me out of work mode.

"Yes?" I looked up from my computer.

"Do you make *this* much money every month?" Your eyes were huge with curiosity as you held up the vision board.

A lump grew in my throat. "Where did you find that?" I asked, trying to gather my composure.

"Behind the couch. It must have fallen back there." You paused for only a second. "So, do you make *this* much money in your business?"

"Do you make this much money every month?" Your eyes were huge with curiosity as you held up the vision board.

There was a bit of pride in your hopeful question, and as it broke my heart, I could feel the shame creeping in.

Not only am I NOT making that much money every month, but I hid that board from you, knowing that if you saw it, you would ask this question. $8,000 per month? Yeah, right, I wish!

"No, Honey. I don't make that much money every month. Not yet." I took a breath and chose my words carefully, "It's my dream board. I want to grow my business to the point where it makes that much money every month, so that we can experience all of those things I wrote around the number." I pointed to the words and pictures depicting family vacations and leisure time we hadn't been able to afford, savings accounts I hadn't been able to open, and other items. It had been a year since I'd started True to Intention, and while some really amazing things had happened, the money wasn't there quite yet.

It was a lot better than last year though…

I'd taken a huge emotional and financial leap by proposing to Lisa my "not quite developed yet" idea of offering a book writing accountability program to those attending her newest event for aspiring speakers and authors. She'd said *'yes,'* and given me just under three weeks to get all of my stuff (logo, website, business cards…oh, *and* curriculum!) together in time for the next event. It was a crazy few weeks (you remember?), but it was the beginning of me seeing how the way had already been paved for my purpose.

It was a good year, my best ever, but we couldn't live on this.

"Oh, okay." You paused, as if you'd felt my shame and were choosing your words, and then your curiosity got the best of you. "Well, how much *do* you make every month?"

"I make enough to pay our bills and do some fun things every once in a while." I tried to assure you that we were well-supported, while hiding the panic that always came up when I thought about money.

"When do you think you'll make $8,000 per month?"

"I'm shooting for it this year — by December." The anxiety was starting to make me sweat. *What if I don't do it? I've had financial goals before, and they didn't happen. What will he think of me if I can't make this happen?*

I tried to assure you that we were well-supported, while hiding the panic that always came up when I thought about money.

"Cool."

"Yes, and maybe you can help me?" Somehow, inspiration had found its way through the panic.

"Sure. How?"

"Well, every time you see that board, think about how fun it will be to get Disneyland passes, take vacations, learn how to ride horses, and whatever else you want to try. Get excited and cheer me on, okay?"

"That's easy," you agreed, as you put the board up on the couch. "It should be up here, right? Where you can see it?"

"Yep. That's a good place for it." You gave me a kiss on your way out of the office, and I stared at the board for a few moments.

No more hiding. It's time to make this happen. I don't know how I'm going to do it, but now I have to. I know he's going to be checking up on me!

I shook my head and smiled at the fact that once again, you were mirroring back possibility with no limits.

It's all so "Why not?" for him. Why couldn't his mom make $8,000 per month? Well…why can't I?

When the Time Arrives

Three weeks later, I found myself in a 3 Days to Cash event with Loral Langemeier, face-to-face with every limiting belief I had about money and the value I bring to this world. In a room full of staff that's made millions of dollars and says, "it's easier to make more money than it is to make enough to get by," I was both excited and completely upside-down again, trying to catch up with the new ideas. And, to make it more fun — NOT! — I was being challenged about my pricing.

"That guy charges people $97 to help them write their books in 30 days." I followed the woman's finger to be polite. "Why do you charge so much for your program?" She was simply just curious.

My heart and mind raced. *How is that possible? He must just be helping them write bullet-list books.* In just a few moments, I had uncovered one of my branding factors.

"I charge more because I help people write trans-formational books — books that combine their personal journeys and their expertise. It takes quite a bit of time to help them get clear, structured, and ready to write."

"Oh, yes, that does sound different than what he does."
We finished the conversation, and as I watched her scurry
off to make another connection, I thought about my
answer.

Yes, I do help them get clear and structured, but they are not
writing enough. They need time away to do all of the homework,
get clear, and write. What if I took them away to a retreat center
for a few days? We could probably get six months of work done
in three days with a small group.

"Amanda!" Ursula's voice broke into my thoughts. "They
are relentless about signing me up for Loral's Big Table
and..." I focused all of my attention on Ursula and helping
her get clear enough to make a decision about whether the
Table was her next step. After some strategizing, she signed
up, and we celebrated that evening and turned in early so
we would be ready for the third day of training. But I woke
up completely undone after an extremely intense dream:

> Loral had walked up to me and said, "So, are you
> coming to the Table with her?" (meaning Ursula)
>
> "Ummmm... Well, I'd love to, but no, not now."
>
> "Why not?"
>
> "I don't have any cash or plastic to make an
> investment like that right now. Maybe next year."

Leaning forward, she started in with all of the reasons I should just 'say *yes* and figure out how.'

"Yes, well, I know it's my next step. I prayed for someone who could help me shift my Money Conversation, and you showed up within a month of that prayer. I just can't do it right at this moment..."

We went back and forth in my dream until my alarm jolted me awake.

Ursula could tell I was shaken, and I told her all about the dream while we got ready, finishing with, "This has to be a breakthrough year with the money. I know this is my calling, and I made more money last year than ever before; but 'my net' could disappear at any moment, and the business has to be able to support us." My voice trembled at the reality I shared out loud for the very first time.

My voice trembled at the reality I shared out loud for the very first time.

"Well, you have already taken the leap and partnered with Lisa. Why not ask big and see what they can do about a payment plan? If it's supposed to happen, it will."

"Yeah, I'm just going to focus on calming the heck down before I get back to that room…"

We finished getting ready, and three hours later, I was standing calmly in the back of the training room when Loral walked up and said, "So, are you coming to the Table with her?"

"Ummmm… Well, I'd love to, but no, not now." *Holy crap! Did she just walk up to me and say the same exact words she said in my dream?!?*

"Why not?"

"I don't have any cash or plastic to make an investment like that right now. Maybe next year." *Oh my goodness. This is the same conversation!!!*

Leaning in, she made the same case she'd made in my dream just three hours before — literally word for word.

"Loral, this is the second time we've had this conversation."

She looked at me puzzled and waited for an explanation.

"I had a dream last night. We had this conversation."

She smiled, "Well, *that* sounds like a sign."

"Yeah, no kidding. Look, I know I'm supposed to say *'yes.'*

I just do not see *how* right now. But I promise, as soon as the money shows up, I'll sign on that dotted line. Clearly, it's a 'meant to be.'"

But holy cow! How will I pay for it? The down payment alone is twice as much as I make a month right now.

I said *'yes'* to the smaller level of coaching before I left that day, knowing that I had to put some money where my intention was, and told her assistant I'd be calling as soon as I could move to the Big Table.

Ready

Two weeks later, I was asked to facilitate a workshop for a small group, and they offered me the exact amount I needed to make my down payment for the Big Table.

Now what are the chances? I guess this means I AM READY?

I called to make my deposit, and when I got off the phone with the sales person, I could feel the conflict happening. There was a part of me that was terrified to make a commitment to such a huge monthly payment and that

> *But there was this other part of me that knew it was time. I was ready.*

didn't believe that I was even capable of sitting at the Big Table with people who think that "it's fun and easy to make money."

Now that's a belief I'd like to have!

But there was this other part of me that knew that it was time. I was ready. The dream was just a confirmation that I was being directed toward the next step.

As I sat there rocking back and forth in my chair, I glanced at the picture of you on my desk and recalled a few early childhood moments when you had shared that same type of knowing and caught me totally off-guard…

We were driving home from the store when you were almost three years old. You were in your toddler seat, looking out the window when it occurred to you, "Mommy, I think I'm ready for school."

"Really?" I looked out the passenger window and smiled when I saw a school bus.

He's ready to hang out with the big kids.

"Yes."

You were so very sure about your decision, but because I wasn't sure you knew what you were saying, or *if I was ready* for you to go to school, I didn't take action right away... until you reminded me a week later. "Mommy, I'm ready for school. When can I start?"

You knew you were ready, and over the years, you have done this over and over again. Remember when you just decided to start swimming? You weren't even trying to learn, and then one day, you just took off your floaties and did it.

And because you were always ready, I hardly ever saw you experience anxiety stepping into the new phase.

Not like me. I thought back to the night before I took Lisa's stage as the Founder of True to Intention, when my anxiety was taking over: "Aaron, if you had a friend who was going to school for the first time and feeling really nervous about it, what would you say to encourage him?" (I bet you didn't know I was asking you for advice for myself, did you? I do it a lot!)

"Be brave. Use your imagination. And ask for help." You said it with so much confidence, I almost laughed out loud at the simple wisdom that just flew out of you.

"That's great advice! Thanks!" I kissed you goodnight and went to bed, choosing bravery and imagination.

Testing & Strengthening Our Wings

A few weeks after I made my first payment for the Big Table, things went totally upside-down. When the butterflies come out, they're upside-down for a bit, right? Well, *all* of my fears and limiting beliefs about money started to come up with a vengeance and began creating chaos. My merchant services froze thousands of dollars for weeks, a few clients delayed their payments, and…well, you get the picture. It wasn't pretty, and I was definitely questioning my decision. *Was I really ready? Is this just a test?*

> "Be brave. Use your imagination. And ask for help." You said it with so much confidence.

And as always, there was an experience with you that helped me to see it and move through it more quickly.

"Mom, I need to go to the store and get some erasers and pencil stoppers."

"You're out of erasers?"

"Oh no, I have some for me. I'm just starting this eraser business at school. My teacher gave everyone play money, and we are buying and selling each other's stuff. It's super fun."

Mmmm…sounds like the entrepreneur bug is contagious! At seven years old? How fun!

I stopped folding clothes for a minute to dig for some more information. "How did you decide on erasers and pencil stoppers?"

"Well, the kids are using their pencils and making mistakes all of the time. Plus, the girls *really* like the sparkly pencil stoppers. They pay *big* money for those."

He already knows his market and what it wants. Smart!

I couldn't hold back the giggle. "Well, okay, I was already planning on going to the store tonight. You can come with me."

When we got to the store, I found what I needed quickly, and then we ran to the office supply aisle. I watched you grab several packages of erasers and stoppers and put them in the cart.

"Wow, you have enough money to pay for *all* of those?"

"Ummm...I don't know." The concern washed over your face as you realized that I was encouraging you to take responsibility for your business. You took a deep breath, suddenly feeling limited by what was in, or not in, your wallet.

Ugh, I hate that feeling. And honestly, I hated to watch you feel it. In fact, it triggered all my lame money beliefs, and they flew out of my mouth without warning.

"It's hard work to earn money, isn't it? Makes you want to not spend it so lightly?"

The minute I said it, I wanted to retract it. *Oh my goodness! Here I am, angry that I have this dumb "have to work hard for money belief" that has me*

Here I am, angry that I have this dumb "have to work hard for money belief" that has me working like a dog, and I just heaped it on him. How can I undo this?

working like a dog and trying to shift it in my own life, and I just heaped it on him. How can I undo this?

I watched you sadly but calmly work out a solution, making decisions out loud about your market (buyers), the demand (what they wanted most), and your capital (what you had to spend to get the business started).

Amazing. How did he learn all of this? And how am I going to undo what I just did, so he doesn't end up a struggling entrepreneur?

When you were done working it all out, we headed for the cash register, and I prayed for guidance. Just before we got there, I noticed a sign that said, "Buy one and get a $20 gift card" and looked up to see that it was for one of those electronic toothbrushes that your dad really wanted.

That's it! I grabbed the toothbrush and threw it in the cart, feeling grateful that there was a way for me to demonstrate that what I'd said wasn't completely true.

"Honey, let me pay for my stuff first." My excitement faded a bit when I looked over and saw your shoulders slumped. You were clearly upset about the situation.

"Okay." You pulled out your wallet and all of your money just to get ready, and I distracted you with a request to choose a pack of gum while I asked the clerk if I could get that $20 gift card right away. She nodded quietly, somehow intuiting that I was up to some serious mommy stuff.

"Here you go, Kiddo!" I handed you the gift card.

"What's this?" You looked very confused.

"Just give it to the lady before you use your cash." I smiled and waited for the moment.

"Okay, young man," the clerk started, "your total is $3.27."

You stared at her, and then at me, as if to ask for help. I just smiled.

"It's only $3.27 for all of this?" You pointed at the bag of erasers and stoppers.

"Yes, after the gift card." The clerk smiled at you and then nodded at me, clearly enjoying this moment.

You shook your head, still not fully understanding and handed her the money. When the transaction was complete, you grabbed your bag, got real close to me, and whispered, "What happened?"

"Well, Big Man. That card I handed you had $20 on it." I smiled, still waiting for it to register.

"And you gave it to me?" Your sparkly eyes told me you were beginning to get it.

"Yes, because I didn't tell you *the whole truth* back there." I paused, making sure you were looking in my eyes. "Money doesn't just come from work. Sometimes, it just comes — like a gift for a birthday, or just because someone sees what you are up to and believes in you." I smiled and looked down at the bag to indicate that I believed in you and your business. "You are obviously a little businessman, and I want to support you and help you be successful. Part of that is asking you to take responsibility for it (like I've had to do in paying for all of my coaching), and part of that is offering extra support (like I've been given through some of my amazing coaches and people who believe in me)."

"Yes, because I didn't tell you the whole truth back there." I paused, making sure you were looking in my eyes.

"Thanks, Mom," and as if to relieve my concerns that I had limited you with my beliefs, you finished, "I'm going to make *a lot* of money with these. It will be so easy!"

You reached up to kiss my cheek to let me know you really got it.

What if it could be easy? What if the breakthrough and the wing training was the hard part?

6

Trusting the Wind

"And your ears shall hear a word behind you, saying, 'This is the way, walk in it, when you turn to the right or when you turn to the left."

Anonymous, *Holy Bible*

"We have all a better guide in ourselves, if we would attend to it, than any other person can be."

Jane Austen

"I think they are ready, Mommy." Your expression was a mixture of excitement and sadness.

"I think you're right, Buddy."

You had been hanging out with the butterflies for almost an hour before you realized it was time to let them go.

"Why don't you come out first, show them how to get out, and then you can hold the door open?"

You nodded and very carefully crawled back out of the bungalow. As soon as you pulled the door open, one of the butterflies followed you out and floated onto a nearby flower.

"Look. He did it." Your proud grin was almost too much to bear.

He seriously feels the same way about these butterflies as I feel about him.

"Yes, look at how brave he is. He just jumped right out there, while the others seem to be taking their time."

> "Looks like the wind is helping them fly. They only have to flap a little, and then they float along the breeze. Isn't that amazing, Aaron?"

"Maybe they're scared." The furrow in your brow made me smile.

You are such a little lover.

"Maybe, or maybe they need to strengthen their wings a little more."

It took the other two a while to find their way out of the bungalow, and both of us were surprised by how they floated between flowers and then back to you for a few minutes. It really did appear to be an expression of gratitude.

They took their time moving from flower to flower, but it wasn't until the breeze picked up that they took longer flights to the other side of the garden.

"Looks like the wind is helping them fly. They only have to flap a little and then they float along the breeze. Isn't that amazing, Aaron?"

You nodded your agreement. We watched them fly and float around the garden for another thirty minutes before they did one final circle around you and took off out of the garden.

"Goodbye, butterflies. Come back and visit us." You didn't try to hide the sadness in your voice, but I could tell you were proud too. Your little friends had grown up quite beautifully and taken off to do what butterflies do.

"Mommy, can I bury the one that died?" You had reached back into the bungalow with a big leaf and scraped up what was left of the poor butterfly.

"Yes, Buddy. Do you want help?"

"No, I got him. I will be right back."

I watched you carefully dig the hole and very gently place the butterfly in the dirt. When you covered it up and patted the dirt, it was like you left your sadness there.

"Okay, Mommy. Can we order more eggs?"

"Of course. I can do that today, but you know those butterflies you just set free are going to be laying some soon too. I bet we see them again."

"I hope so."

Whispers on the Wind

Shortly after I paid for the Big Table, in the midst of the cash freeze crisis, I was inspired to create a Jumpstart Your Message Retreat for aspiring authors — where I could take them away from their busy lives for three days, get them clear on their message, structure it, brand it, and then move them into an ongoing coaching program.

I'd learned from Ursula that the best way to do anything was to just get out there and do it, so I stressed about the format and pricing for only one week before putting it out there. LOL!

Without too much effort, I had six people sign up for the retreat.

Yes! I am on track. Just need to stay focused. The money piece will sort itself out.

The day arrived, and my heart raced while I set up the Guest House and waited for them.

What if I can't do this? What if they just paid me all this money and they don't get what they are coming here to get?

I was right in the middle of talking myself off the ledge when Tami walked in. She was the only one I didn't know very much about. At the very last minute, one of the participants had called to see if there was room for her and worked out all of the details between us.

I looked up when she walked in the door and caught my breath. She was clearly upset — wide-eyed, red-faced, and breathless.

"Where's my room?" she asked without so much as a greeting.

"It's number five, second door on the left." I pointed in the direction.

She dragged all of her stuff to her room and shut the door behind her. (She and I still debate whether she actually slammed the door, or if it was just my anxiety making it sound that loud.)

Oh my goodness! This is not good! I pulled myself together enough to greet everyone else as they walked in, and we got started.

The whole weekend was amazing, except that Tami seemed paralyzed. She probably said a total of ten words

The whole weekend was amazing, except that Tami seemed paralyzed.

the first two days, and wasn't completing any of the exercises or interacting with the other participants.

What are you going to do? She's not going to get what she came for. You're not delivering on your promises. She's going to demand her money back. Maybe this was all a really bad idea!

It was the last day of the retreat, and everyone else had completed the exercises. As Tami walked to the front of the room, everyone held their breath and prayed for a breakthrough.

"My heart, O God, hungers after you…" The tears welled in everyone's eyes as she sang a song that had clearly been conceived in pain and longing for a deeper connection with God. Time stood still, and when the song was over, she shared her story and the message that she wanted to share with the world.

Stunned, everyone in the room was silent. Suddenly uncomfortable, Tami curtsied and sat down. Quickly snapping back into my role, I asked her to stand back up and asked the others to reflect back what they'd heard. One of the ladies said that as Tami had been singing, another song had come to mind and asked if she could share it. Tami nodded, and when the woman finished the first verse, Tami took over. When she finished the song, she dropped into a heap of tears in the middle of the room. Face down in child's pose, she wept. And the room wept with her.

I leaned on the wall in front of me and let the tears fall.

"Amanda, this is your real work…"

It had been a long time since I'd heard that still, small voice.

"It's not about the books. It's about them. They need a safe space and someone to walk with them on this journey, so they can heal as they write their stories."

There was a pause, and the room was silent, except for Tami's quiet sobs.

"But Amanda, you are standing by the door. You can say 'no' if you want to."

> "Amanda, this is your real work…" It had been a long time since I'd heard that still, small voice.

I looked up and was shocked to see that I was actually right next to the door.

I can't leave. There's a woman in a heap of pain on the floor. I have no idea how I'm going to do this, but I'm not leaving.

"Just keep listening. I've brought you here. I am not going anywhere."

I smiled, wiped the tears away, and stepped into my purpose…listening and trusting.

What if that's all I ever needed to do?

Quietly Waiting & Watching

As I reflected on the retreat over the next few days, I kept coming back to that moment by the door. It had been almost fifteen years since I'd heard that voice, hearing guidance and direction for a task in the moment. I mean, it had been obvious since the day Lisa had walked into the Sizzler behind me, and I'd gone to her workshop and written my autobiography that I had been at the center of a divine intervention, but…

> *I only knew it in my head. I had a lot of evidence that God had been working behind the scenes, but…*

I only knew it in my head. I had a lot of *evidence* that God had been working behind the scenes, but my rage, depression, and pain had choked that still, small voice to a whisper that I couldn't hear above the pain and chaos that *was* my life for almost a decade. There *had* been moments where I'd felt the presence of God — during your first prayer, on the way home from that transformational workshop, etc. — but the real-time guidance hadn't happened since I was sixteen on the kitchen floor, rocking my baby sister, asking God to tell me what He wanted to share with my Bible class, and seeing and feeling the unconditional love He wanted *me* to understand.

I don't want to run this business or facilitate transformation for others without that real-time guidance.

So, in addition to continuing my work with some of the angels who had shown up to help me clear out and replace negative patterns of thinking, feeling, and behaving, I started to create more quiet time to listen for that direction.

By the time the second retreat happened a few months later, I was getting very specific direction, all the way down to which exercises I should use for this group. I didn't always understand the direction, but I kept listening, and little miracles happened to confirm it.

For example, at that next retreat, I was guided to insert a painting exercise. I had no idea why or what they were supposed to paint until the morning of the retreat, but when we did the exercise, I was shocked in the moment and well beyond the retreat. The exercise not only gave me the information and insight I needed to coach them through the transformation more effectively, but it sparked a journey for one of the participants. She uncovered a dormant talent and love for painting, and is now selling her masterpieces for hundreds of dollars.

What if all this is happening because I started listening?

Your Own Wind

"Mom, I don't want to go to school anymore."

"What? Why? I thought you were enjoying school."

"I was, but I'm not anymore." Your voice was so full of stress, I put my computer down and sat next to you.

"Honey, what's happening?"

"Some of the kids are being mean to me. They are saying that their parents won't let them talk to me because I'm not part of their family, and my teacher won't do anything about it."

Oh no! It's like he's living through my second grade year?!?!

My first instinct was to yank you out of the school, and give your teacher a piece of my mind on our way out. But my emotions were so intense that I knew I had to go to some of my mentors for a reality check before taking action. And, of course, I didn't like what they said because it meant watching you suffer through the process of figuring it out: "He has to handle the bullies. If he doesn't learn how to exert his own power, he will always deal with bullies…at other schools and…"

They didn't have to finish that sentiment. I knew the end of that story, as I had lived it. *He will dim his light more and more and more, until the real him goes missing…*

Not under my watch…

"Aaron, I can't pull you out of school." It was a few days after our first conversation about the bullies.

"Why?" Your lip quivered.

"Honey, listen, I don't like this either. I really want to, but there are bullies at other schools too. And here's the thing about bullies — they only pick on the kids they think are too weak to fight back. They are usually being bullied at home by a parent, or a sibling, and are tired of losing against the 'stronger person' in their lives, so they bully kids that appear to be weak in order to feel powerful."

He will dim his light more and more and more, until the real him goes missing… Not on my watch…

"Really? You mean they are being bullied, too?" You were shocked to hear that their power ended somewhere.

"It's very possible. All of the bullies I knew in school, as a student and a teacher, were usually being bullied at home. In fact, I think they are bullies because they don't know any other way to feel powerful. And they don't go after the confident kids, cuz they won't win. So, we have to figure out how you are going to show them who you really are — a strong, kind, and responsible kid. Any ideas?"

> *"Do whatever you need to do, Aaron, but listen to your own voice. Even if you get into trouble... make a mistake... it will be okay."*

We talked about all of the possibilities, and knowing that you had to figure this out on your own, I tried not to give you the answers when you asked, "But what do I do if...? But what if I get into trouble for...?"

"Do whatever you need to do, Aaron, but listen to your own voice. Even if you get into trouble...even if you make a mistake while trying to figure it out... it will be okay. I know you are going to figure this out. You might not get it right the first time, and it may be something that you have to do a few times before you get the results you want, but you have what it takes."

"Okay, Mom. I'll try."

Over the next few weeks, we checked in on your progress. You tried everything you knew how to do, and then one day, I asked you, "What's happening with the bullies?"

And you answered, "You know, I stopped arguing with them, and telling the teacher, and everything else. I just ignored them and hung out with my friend who was being bullied too. And they aren't bothering us as much."

What if that's all it takes — just focusing on what we want and ignoring what we don't?

"Congratulations, Aaron. Sounds like you took a good step. You still want to go to another school?"

"Yeah, my teacher is starting to go crazy. She threw a stapler against the wall the other day. I just don't think it's a good situation anymore."

"Oh dear. I think you're right."

Trusting the Wind

By the time I got to my first Big Table session, I was deeply connected to that still, small voice. I quickly and easily created my 120-day plan for the business and went home to implement it. But after taking the first step, a possibility opened up that I hadn't seen before — an opportunity that required that I leave the plan I'd just written behind and trust my guidance. Several of my coaches discouraged me from diverting from the steps they'd approved; in fact, some of them tried to push me around and tell me that I would fail if I didn't do it their way. But I knew...

I knew that it was safe for me to trust the wind and take flight. And I did. In just a few short months, I had received my first standing ovation for a presentation I'd delivered to an extremely high-level coaching program, designed the Book Production and Messenger Launch Programs, tripled my revenue, been nominated for an award, and become a bestselling author. And even more importantly, life on the home front had begun healing in big ways.

I can hardly believe it! My business is taking off, my marriage is healing, my family is relaxing into this whole journey with me, my community is growing...

How can it get better than this? I wondered to myself, as I sat around the table with my family and waited to see if I'd won the award.

Oh yeah, this next project is going to be the culmination of my six years on this journey. So exciting....

Unfortunately, I called the queasiness in my stomach "butterflies of excitement" when they were really warning signals...

Ignoring the Wind

We had been thoroughly enjoying our family vacation, and it was all fun and giggles, until the loud slap. You'd tickled her so much, that she had flailed and mindlessly slapped your leg. It was so loud, everyone in the room stopped and looked to see you and your aunt facing each other, both of you searching for what to do or say.

It was so loud, everyone in the room stopped and looked to see you and your aunt facing each other.

"Aaron, I'm sorry. Here, slap me back, as hard as you can, and we'll be even." She put her leg down in front of you and waited.

You looked at her leg and then at me across the room, as if asking what to do. But I was paralyzed. All I could do was shrug my shoulders at you, affirming to you that this was *your* decision, not mine.

With everyone staring at you, you raised your arm and slapped her leg pretty hard. And then you quickly walked over to me, looked me straight in the eyes with tears brimming, and asked, "Can we go back to the room *right now*?"

Without waiting for my answer, you opened the door and walked down to our hotel room. And I ran to keep up, still not knowing what to say.

As soon as I unlocked the door, you pushed past me, ran to the bathroom, locked yourself in, and started screaming.

"Aaron, are you okay?"

"No!" you screamed.

"Are you hurt? Do you need an ice pack?" I screamed back through the door to make sure you heard me.

The screaming didn't stop, so I tried again. "Aaron, are you hurt? What can I do to help you?"

You flung the door open, threw your arms down to your sides, and stomped your feet. "No, Mom! My body doesn't

hurt! I feel like a bad person!!!!! You can't do *anything!*"
The pain emanating from your body and eyes was almost
too much for me to bear, and my legs went weak.

"Why?" was all I could get out.

"Because I *knew* I shouldn't slap her, and I did it anyway. I feel like a bad person!"

You fell in a heap on the bathroom floor, and I let you cry it out, but the tears wouldn't stop. After a while, I asked you, "What can we do?"

"I want...to tell her...I'm sorry." You stammered through the tears.

"Okay, do you want me to go back to her room with you?"

You shook your head.

"Do you want me to ask her to come over here?"

You shook your head again.

I was trying to figure out a solution when you asked, "Can I use your phone?"

> *You flung the door open, threw your arms down to your sides, and stomped your feet. "No, Mom! I feel like a bad person!!!!"*

"Sure…" I handed you my phone and watched you take some deep breaths, brush away the tears, and text your apology: "Lyssie, this is Aaron. I'm very sorry I slapped you. I love you. Aaron."

As soon as you finished the text, you fell back on your pillow and let out the most painful sobs I've ever heard you cry. You were inconsolable for the next twelve hours, crying through your sleep. Your heart was absolutely broken…

As I lay there in the bed, my momma heart hurting with yours, I thought about how paralyzed I'd felt in that room.

Why didn't I say anything? Could I have saved you from this pain?

Almost as soon as I asked the question, I saw the gift in the situation and prayed for a way to help you understand it.

The next morning, when you woke up, you jumped into bed next to me and whispered, "Mom, I still feel so bad."

"I know, Sweetie. I'm sorry it hurts so bad, but I'm really glad you are learning this at eight years old."

"Learning what?" You looked up at me through puffy eyes.

"Well, you said last night that you *knew* the right thing to do, and you didn't do it, right?"

"Yeah…" Another little sniffle helped to make your point.

"That feeling or knowing, that little voice — the one that said, 'don't hit her back' — is *in* you to help you make the best possible choices for yourself as you go through life. You looked at me to see if it was okay to hit her, but you already knew the right answer. Right?"

"Right…"

"So, why did you do it?"

"Well, I thought everyone in the room thought I should."

"I thought so. That happens to a lot of kids."

"It does?"

"Yes, and sometimes, they get so used to looking outside of themselves (at parents, teachers, and friends) for what they should and shouldn't do that they end up not hearing their own voice

"That feeling or knowing, that little voice…is in you to help you make the best possible choices for yourself…"

anymore. And then what happens when the adult or the friend tells them to do something wrong or dangerous, and they have learned to disregard their own voice?"

"They do it?"

"Yeah, that happened to me."

"It did?"

"Yep, and I made some decisions that I knew were not the best decisions for me. And I suffered some pretty steep consequences."

"Like what?"

I shared some of the decisions and consequences and watched your eyes widen with surprise. When I knew I had made my point, I asked, "So the lesson here is…?"

"I know the right thing to do…" Your voice was still a whimper.

"Yes, and…?"

"And if I don't listen, I'm going to feel like this again."

"Yes, and I am thankful that you learned it at eight years old. I want you to remember this, Aaron. Remember that little voice. Remember this feeling. You will be able to avoid a lot of the pain that kids, teenagers, and adults suffer if you practice listening to your own voice."

You nodded in agreement and fell back to sleep on my pillow. As I watched you sleep, I thought about all of the times I hadn't listened to my own voice and feelings.

Too bad it didn't occur to me then that I was having those feelings again. Maybe I would have paid attention to them.

The Whispers Don't Lie

I sat across from three of my friends who were shaking with fury and disbelief on my behalf. They had just witnessed one of the deepest hurts I've ever endured unfold right before their eyes. My head was swirling and my body was numb with shock.

This project was supposed to be the culmination and celebration of six years of transformational work. What happened?

"I can't believe they would do this to you. This is *so* low!"

I listened as they shared all of the details I hadn't seen myself. This person did this. This person ignored that. This person said this. This person said that.

Oh heavens…could it be? I drifted back over the last eighteen months of interaction with them, trying to remember the details of the last few conversations. *Didn't I see this coming?*

"Amanda?"

"Yes?"

"Did you hear that?"

"Yes, I heard enough of it." I took a deep breath before continuing, "And now, I have to take responsibility for it."

"What?!?!?!" All three of them nearly screamed in tandem.

"*I'm probably going to be raging mad and extremely hurt. But I think I set myself up…*"

"Don't get me wrong. I'm horrified, and when the numbness wears off, I'm probably going to be raging mad and extremely hurt. But I think I set myself up…"

"What do you mean?" They couldn't believe their ears.

I started to tell them about the interactions and conversations of the last eighteen months, and as I spoke, it only became more apparent to me that something had been wrong for a while,

and I had found a way to totally ignore all of the big red
flags that had popped up.

I had given my time, my love, and my expertise, and it had
been wonderful and beautiful for a long time. *But over the
past eighteen months, the relationship definitely shifted.* There'd
been moments when I'd felt like they didn't have my best
interest at heart, or the reciprocity of the relationship was
no longer equal.

"And I ignored every warning flag..."

We sat in silence as I considered the total impact of my
inattention to my own voice and guidance. By continually
discounting my gut feelings, I had compromised my
financial well-being (losing tens of thousands of dollars),
my community (that had to make sense
of the conflict between what they were
feeling and what I'd communicated to
them), and my own heart (losing one of
my favorite people in the whole world).
All because I ignored my feelings until
it was too late...

*The deepest betrayal was mine. I should
have honored my own voice.*

*The deepest
betrayal was
mine. I
should have
honored my
own voice.*

Letting Go & Trusting the Wind

The grief process was intense once the shock wore off. I raged, I cried, I ranted, and I felt a big gaping hole in my life. I leaned on close friends, I worked with my mentors, and I did my best to love myself as I handled it all so imperfectly.

"Amanda, you don't need them." Ursula's voice was full of compassion.

"I know." I said it without much enthusiasm.

"Do you?" Now it was firm.

"I think so. I guess it's true that I thought I needed them to go somewhere in the business, and I guess the money was attached to that. But on the other side of the grief, I can see the truth. And maybe that's the gift in all of this…"

"What exactly?"

"The lesson here is not only to listen to my own voice and trust my feelings, but to realize that at the end of the day, my well-being — personally, professionally, emotionally, financially, physically, etc. — is dependent on me and my divine connection. All of this success and expansion for the last year is not because of the tight business plan and formula that my coaches handed me, or the relationships I cultivated..." I paused, trying to find the words, "It's the direct result of me reconnecting with and trusting that still, small voice again. I learned how to trust the wind and fly, and I'm going to do it again."

7

Butterfly Impact

"By focusing on yourself you limit the
amount of energy that you output,
because there is only one you.
Yet by focusing on others you multiply the
amount of energy you output by the number
of others with whom you do so...
Everything that you create, you experience..."

Neale Donald Walsch

"Mommy, I think I saw one of my butterflies today."

I looked over to see you closing the screen door behind you.

"Did you? How did you know it was one of yours?" I put the spatula down and gave you my full attention.

"It was the same color, and it came really close — like it knew me."

"That's really cool, Aaron. I never thought that butterflies could feel or express gratitude, but it really seems like they are, doesn't it?" I went back to cooking as I awaited your answer.

"Yeah, and then he landed on a flower and stayed there for a few minutes. I wonder if he left some magic eggs for us…"

I looked up to see your eyes smiling as big as your mouth was.

"I wonder how many…"

"Well, I hear that butterflies can lay up to 100 eggs at a time."

"Wow! And then those will be butterflies, and then lay 100 eggs? That's *a lot* of butterflies."

"That's right. Because you took such good care of three butterflies, there could be 300 eggs in our backyard."

Your big eyes gazed out into the garden, clearly in awe of the possibility.

Daring to Dream Big!

"Good evening! Wow! Look at this room! You know, I imagined standing up here and saying something like, '*It's just like I dreamed it would be,*' but that's simply *not* true! This…" my hands extended toward the room packed with more than two hundred eager, smiling faces, "…is *way* beyond my dreams!"

I paused, just to breathe in the moment, realizing what a perfectly Divine Set-up this was for the message I'd been inspired to deliver.

"You see, this is what happens when you *dare to dream*... Seven months ago, this event was just an inspiration — a crazy idea that made perfect sense and no sense at all..."

As people continued to trickle in and stood along the walls, I shared the story of how this event had all been inspired and unfolded.

I was listening to a two-week-old recorded call during which Lisa had offered to keynote and sign our co-authored *Unbreakable Spirit* books at only six events.

Well, that's a no-brainer. I mean, we are not just co-authors. We partner to help aspiring authors write books, for goodness' sake.

Suddenly, a flood of possibilities downloaded: *What if this could be a True to Intention event — where I could launch some of my authors on the stage next to myself and a six-time* New York Times *Bestselling Author? Wouldn't that be awesome?!? Wow...I bet they'd get those books done fast.*

> "You see, this is what happens when you dare to dream..."

But by the end of the recording, I heard her say that six co-authors had already texted her names and dates and, remember, that was *two weeks* earlier. But I didn't care. I knew this event was supposed to happen, so I called Lisa and made a big request. And, of course, she said 'yes.'

And then came the upside-down…

Crap! How are we going to produce the books in time? I have a team to polish them, but how are we going to get them designed, printed, and published?

I was almost sick to my stomach, thinking about how some of my previous authors had struggled desperately to complete the final stages of their book journey. And then it hit me.

Don't I already know people who could do all of that? Hmmmm…a Messenger Launch Program?

And then the magic happened. The team came together. The system was created. The authors took the leap, made the investment, and wrote their books in less than two months. The editing, the design, the websites…it all got done.

"And here we are…" I continued, determined to inspire audience members to dare to dream again. "But here's what I really want you to get: *I had no idea what it would take to make this dream happen when I said 'yes' to it seven months ago.* I had no idea who all would be involved or that the hidden blessing was a substantial jump in my revenue, an amazing program that could save my clients from the pain of self-publishing, and…a packed house."

The tears welled, and I took a deep breath around the lump in my throat, "All I had was the *knowing* that it had to happen, and the *belief* that I had everything I needed (within and around me) to do it. It hasn't all been easy. There have been more than a fair share of tears and breakdowns," I paused and smiled as several of the most painful ones crossed my mind, "but take a moment and look around this room. This was just a dream seven months ago. Only *one* of the books you see featured tonight was actually fully written and produced when I said 'yes' to this. And look…at the impact of one dream."

Uncovering the BIG WHY

What a night that was! Our family, my mentors, my

colleagues, my community...all in one place, celebrating transformation, feeling inspired, and daring to dream their own dreams again.

I watched your face closely throughout the event, praying that you would be excited and inspired to dream big, and then I thought about how it was really *you* who started this whole journey.

You were my BIG WHY, Aaron.

You were my BIG WHY, Aaron, and that horrible moment we shared in the parking lot...while I wish it had never happened and that I had been a healthier mommy for you, I can now see it as a bittersweet gift. The desire to see you live an unlimited life, mixed with the pain of hurting you in such a deep way, catalyzed a journey that has not only healed me and our family, it is being used to help so many others heal their lives and step into their dreams and purpose.

Your face beamed bright from the audience all night (except when you went out to play with your cousin).

I asked you the next day, "So what did you think of the event?"

Your answer surprised me. "Mom, I'm so proud of you for getting into that dress!"

I laughed so hard. *Everything you witnessed last night, and the part that stands out is me fitting into the dress!* But then I got it — that was important to you because *you* were partly responsible for it. I'd empowered you to get in my face every time you saw me eating too many potato chips or French fries for the last two months, and oh my goodness, did you!

I love that…the part that stood out to him was the part that he could take some ownership of, and yet he said he was proud of me. Mmmm…

What if that's what this life is all about — helping each other reach our goals?

Remembering What Really Matters

I looked at my phone buzzing on my desk and smiled before answering, "Ruben! Hello!"

"Amanda, how are you?" His voice was full of life and sincerely curious.

"I'm doing pretty well, Ruben. And you?"

"Life is beaauuutiful!" he exclaimed. I smiled and was

ready to ask how his book was coming when he interjected another question, "How's business?"

"It's good. Last year was about huge expansion, and this year's been about letting go of mentors, colleagues, team members, and even clients who are not in alignment with the vision. It's been painful, but I see the gifts in it."

"That's good, Amanda. It's all part of the business and life cycle. Sounds like you're doing great."

"Thanks, Ruben. That means a lot coming from you. Now what can I do for *you*? I hope this call has to do with your book!"

"Yes, it does. I'm going to finish it by the end of next month, and then, can we plan to meet and discuss what it will look like to get it ready for print?"

"Absolutely. When…?"

We calendared time, but before we met, he found out that his cancer had returned with a vengeance. They gave him six months, and yet he conjured the energy to finish the book and visit with me to discuss next steps.

We talked about the manuscript, the possible titles, and his desire for a bestseller campaign before his wife left to pick up their son. But when she had closed the door behind her, he leaned close and almost whispered, "Amanda, I know you are *really* busy working on your own book, and Ursula's, and probably others, but…" I took a deep breath, somehow intuiting where this was going. "Well, this morning, the doctors said that I only have thirty days of lucidity left, so I'm hoping you can review the content and get everything you need from me…soon…just in case they're right this time."

"Of course we will." I looked down at the table to gather my thoughts. When I finally looked up, I had to ask, "Ruben, I can't even imagine that conversation…thirty days…?"

My voice trailed off, and he picked up, "Yeah. I'm going to try to prove them wrong again, but just in case, I'm working on this list of things that has to happen before I go. I'm going to marry my wife again in a church, tie up a few things with the business, and complete this book…" He paused and inhaled deeply. "It's my legacy…" Now he looked down at the table and pressed his fingers together in front of him. "I have learned and lived so much. Wouldn't it be irresponsible for me to go without leaving it here for others?"

> *"Well, this morning, my doctors said that I only have thirty days left…"*

All I could do was smile and nod, and let the tears fall. *Thirty days…That dream I had about having one year left was intense, but thirty days? What would I do if I only had thirty days?*

> "*I have learned and lived so much. Wouldn't it be irresponsible for me to go without leaving it here for others?*"

Suddenly, clarity took over. "Ruben, would you be the keynote speaker for my Dare to Dream event in March?"

"Absolutely, if…" He paused, and asked, "What do you want me to say?"

"Well, this conversation about leaving a legacy means a lot to me. Two years ago, I had a dream that I only had one year left, and when I woke up, I knew that the one thing I had to do was make sure my son knew how he had changed my life. Wouldn't it be irresponsible for me to go without leaving what I've learned for him?"

He smiled, clearly happy that I was using his words.

"I'm going to finish *Upside-Down Mommy*, make it a bestseller, and invite people to a life-changing weekend of dreaming, transformation, and celebration. I don't want it to be about me and my book, but about the message of what's possible when we choose healing, self-love, and purpose...when we choose to leave a legacy."

"Amanda, I would be honored, but..."

I cut him off, "Ruben, let's record an interview-style keynote, and then if something happens..." Now I couldn't finish. The words caught in my throat.

"Sounds like a plan. How's next week?"

"It's great! I'll send you the questions, set up the crew to record it, and ask my team to drop everything and slide this book to the front of the production line."

I gave him a hug and left.

Thirty days... I let the tears roll down my face all the way home, as I made decisions about my life.

What if I only had thirty days? What if I lived like that? What would I do differently? How would I spend my time?

What Breaks Your Heart?

By the time I got home from Ruben's, I'd identified and already mentally eliminated the stuff that didn't really matter in my business plan and my schedule. And over the next week, I let go of those items and the team members and clients who were creating more crazy than anything else. And…I moved with velocity toward my goals.

Somehow the conversation of *"thirty days"* helped me to not only eliminate everything that wasn't in alignment with my purpose, but to remember where this all started…with this message for moms — the message that became very clear when I asked myself the questions, "What value do I have to give the world?" and "What breaks my heart?"

There was nothing that broke my heart more than walking into public restrooms and hearing mothers hurt, limit, and shame their children with careless words. Of course, I completely understood being disconnected and out-of-control after the parking lot incident, but oh my goodness…I don't know how many bathrooms I ran out of with tears streaming down my face. I wanted to take every child home with me and tell them how beautiful, wonderful, and powerful they are.

If I only had thirty days left, there would be no way that I would leave the planet without getting the message on paper. It's my purpose to do what I can to make sure you always remember who you are...and to help other moms help their children (and themselves) do the same. There is no time to waste...

And of course, I remembered how you had modeled this to me for years — witnessing something that breaks your heart and taking immediate action. Do you remember how insistent you were when you saw "the dogs crying" on the

> *There is no time to waste...*

Humane Society commercials and rush to give me most of your monthly allowance for it? And how many times did you witness my pain and offer a hug or smile? How many times did you see Grandma struggling to feel happy or do something with her crippled hands, and immediately offer to help?

Aaron, what if these things that break our hearts do so because we are meant to do something about them? What if we are designed to be the answers to hurting people's (animals') prayers?

What if you have been modeling powerfully living on purpose since you were born because everything we need to know about living on purpose and leaving a legacy is already inside of us — that magic egg we all have?

Choosing What You Love

"Mom, I don't want to do this anymore." You walked into the laundry room to make your case with a stack of papers in your hand.

"Honey, you said you would, and I agreed to pay you for it."

"I know, but I seriously *hate* shredding papers. Is there anything else I can do to make money?" Your commitment to respect our agreements made me smile, and your exasperation made me giggle quietly.

Oh my goodness! I've been there…

You were just three or four at the time, and you'd poked your head into the bathroom while I was getting ready. "Mom, I don't want to work when I grow up." You were adamant.

"How come, Sweetie?" I asked, feeling a bit of panic rising.

"Because you come home tired and cranky every day. I don't want that."

It felt like a knife through my heart, but I had to tell the truth, "Aaron, you're so smart. I *hate* this job, and *that's* why I feel tired and cranky. I'm not doing what I love to do…"

"You mean, you *could* be doing something you like to do? And you're not?" Your voice was incredulous.

"Well, yeah. That's why I've been in the training program. I'm learning what I need to learn to do that. In the meantime, I'm doing this job to pay the bills."

"Oh…well, I guess if I could do something I *really* like to do…" I'm not sure you finished the sentence as you walked down the hall, but I stayed in the bathroom, took a few deep breaths, and determined that I'd never settle for a situation like this again because I didn't want you to ever think it was the only way.

What if he could grow up believing (with my model reinforcing) that he could choose or create the life and work he loves?

"You mean, you could be doing something you like to do? And you're not?" Your voice was incredulous.

"Well, Honey. What chores would you rather do?" I put down the folded towel and waited for you to answer.

"I could do the laundry, or the dishes, or…"

Wow! He must really hate shredding! I smiled, excited that you actually felt comfortable and empowered enough to ask.

"Okay, you've got it. I'll do the shredding, and you do the dishes. Deal?"

"Deal!" You skipped along to your next job.

It was only a few days later that you walked up to me in the kitchen and said, "Okay, Mom. I'm still going to do all of my chores, but I just want you to know that I'm working for Grandma now. She pays *way* better than you do!"

Oh my goodness. I hope he's not taking advantage of her. She just loves to spoil him. I was ready to challenge you when it occurred to me that what you were *really* doing was making a declaration about the worth of your time and energy.

What if I am meant to help others and live abundantly inside of what I am called to do?

Maintaining Agreements with Love

"Aaron, it's okay for you to stand up for yourself with her."

"But *you* don't." You didn't try to hide the challenge, but it was okay because I'd asked you to keep me honest.

"I know I'm not really great at it yet, but I'm working on it. Maybe we can work on it together?"

I watched you make several attempts at standing up to her over the next few weeks, and I was proud to watch you work it out. The key was staying in a place of respect, and you were really trying when I gave you yet another opportunity to prove that you'd figured it out.

"Mom, what are you doing on my computer? You didn't ask." I jolted upright at the no-nonsense tone of your voice behind me.

I'd opened the computer, knowing that I should've asked. It's a family agreement, right? But instead of taking responsibility, I found myself making excuses, "Well, Grammy needed to see a menu, and my computer is upstairs, and…"

> "*Aaron, you know that the 'normal parent' thing to do is to wonder what you are hiding on your computer...*"

"Mom, close the computer." You were so calm and firm, I had to suppress my smile.

"Okay, I'll go get mine." I ran upstairs to get my computer, and after I'd done everything I needed to do, I asked you to chat with me for a minute.

"Aaron, you know that the 'normal parent' thing to do is to wonder what you are hiding on your computer..." I waited to see your reaction.

You answered with an exasperated sigh but no disrespect, "Mom, I can open my computer and take you through it right now. I don't have anything to hide. I'm just angry that you touched my stuff without asking. It's a family agreement, isn't it?"

"Yes, it is. And I heard my little voice tell me to ask, and I didn't. I'm sorry, Aaron."

"It's okay, Mom. We're good." You kissed me and ran off to play.

And I did the happy mommy dance at the top of the stairs! I'd struggled with boundaries and agreements with mentors, team members, and clients all year, trying to figure out what you just did so easily.

What if it's easier to stay true to intention when there are clear agreements made up front? What if I maintained those agreements with firm love and respect?

Asking & Expecting

It was the longest labyrinth walk ever. It was dark and cold outside, and it felt like the prayer walk that I'd thoroughly enjoyed hundreds of times before had become a never-ending maze. The path hadn't changed a bit, but it felt like it had become twice as long.

When we finally finished and went back into the Guest House, I thought about what a great mirror it was. Everything I was doing felt like *a lot* of hard work.

I am clearly tired of the 'hard work' pattern in my life. But how do I shift it?

As if to answer my question, the next night, you and your daddy came to visit me (like you always do when I'm

*What if
I made
everything
that feels
hard right
now fun
and decided
to skip
through it?*

facilitating a retreat), and I invited you to join us on another labyrinth walk. Something told me the group needed some more time in there, so we went. Little did I know it was really for me.

Stomp. Stomp. Stomp. Stomp. "Darn it. Dang sandal!" Stomp. Stomp. Stomp. Hum. Hum. Hum. You were virtually racing through the labyrinth, stopping now and then to put your sandal back on, unapologetically stepping on and off the path around the people who were going slower, and showing them the way when they were feeling lost. It took everything I had not to laugh out loud as I watched you practically skip your way through an experience that I had called "difficult, long, and frustrating" just the evening before.

What if I made everything that feels hard right now fun and decided to skip through it?

When we stepped out of the labyrinth, you whispered in my ear, "Mom, you know when I am praying in the labyrinth, I say, 'Thank you in advance.'" I act like it's already happened, and then it does."

I was silent for a minute, stunned by the wisdom. "Wow,

Aaron. That's amazing! I think I need to start doing that more."

What if I just expected it to be easy — expected God to supply my every need and guide my every step? What if I just thanked Him in advance? Genius!

Choosing Our Impact

I sat across from Ruben in his beautiful office. We discussed the questions for the interview, and I thanked him again for making time for this.

The video crew arrived and said they needed ten minutes. *Ten minutes... maybe he can jam through some emails or make a phone call.* I got up to leave the office, determined to not take up any more of his precious time than he'd agreed to.

"Amanda, don't leave. We have ten minutes. What do you want to know?"

"What? About the interview? I think we're good."

"No, Amanda. What do *you* want to know? About

business? About life? How can I help *you* today?"

My heart raced. *What do you ask a dying man who is so beloved and so successful?*

I took my time, looking for my most important question. "How does one keep their family healthy and happy while building an empire that helps others in the world?"

> *My heart raced. What do you ask a dying man who is so beloved and so successful?*

He smiled and pressed his fingers together with excitement, "That's really a conversation about Impact and Capacity. You see, too many people focus on increasing their Capacity — how can I make more money, create more time, etc.? — instead of keeping their eyes on their Impact and the outcome they are seeking." He paused and took a labored breath. "But they have it all wrong because when you focus on Impact, and keep your eyes there, Capacity *has* to rise to meet it." He paused to make sure I was following him.

"Yes, Ruben, I know that's true. That's what happened last year in my business! I did insane things that I never thought I could do because I wanted to create a better solution for my clients, and somehow, the team, the information, and the money showed up for everyone involved!"

"That's right..." He smiled, but was interrupted before he could continue.

"Ruben, we're ready." The team member poked her head in, and we stood up and walked into the other room while my mind was still trying to make the connections: *How does this relate to the home and work balance?*

The interview was incredibly inspiring, and after he'd answered all of the questions, I decided to ask him to finish our previous conversation: "Ruben, how do you maintain balance between work and life?"

"Why do you separate them? That's the problem." His quick reply caught me off-guard.

All I could do was stare at him and wait. *Did he just switch from Interviewee to Coach?*

"What if you didn't separate them? What if you just lived in the present moment, choosing to *powerfully* impact every person you interact with? It could be your husband, your son, your clients, or the lady at the drive-thru window."

The minute he finished, I felt a deep shift occur in every cell in my body.

This wasn't a new idea to me. In fact, it's part of what I

What if it isn't about what I "do" in the world as much as about who I "be"?

teach and seek to model — become True to Intention, who you are meant to be, doing what you are meant to do. But he'd mirrored back to me that I was too focused on the "what I do" (Capacity) in both areas of my life, instead of focusing on "being me… everywhere, all the time…a person who can powerfully impact every person who crosses my path" — my true Impact.

What if it isn't about what I "do" in the world as much as it is about who I "be"?

What if it isn't about "making an impact" in the world as much as it is about "choosing the impact" I am making?

Celebrating the Impact

"It doesn't matter what happens. For the first time in a long time, I'm really okay with trusting God no matter what happens. And it's because of what I've learned through this process. I am loved and supported, and it's all good." Her eyes were twinkling and her smile was real, and the tears poured down my face. Unable to speak, let alone continue coaching the group of messengers listening in person and virtually, I took a few deep breaths.

All of my hard work, the time, the breakdowns, the tears, and the upside-down moments…they were all worth it for this. I'd do it all over again, just to see her have this breakthrough.

Eighteen months earlier, this young woman's eyes were dark with sadness and anger, and the smile she wore was plastic. I recognized it because I'd been there. I did everything I could to keep her engaged in the program, holding the space for her as she walked through the loss of two family members, her business, and the dream of having her kidneys healed. And now, the book is almost ready to go to production, and she is transformed.

Yes, this is all worth it.

Later that morning, on the yoga mat, I thought about this beautiful woman's transformation, and the last year, and what has transpired in the business and in my life.

Yes, I had to let go of so many people and so many dreams, but look at what's happening. These books are getting done and changing lives. The messengers are growing businesses and impacting lives, and coming back to train with me at my retreats. And Tami even facilitated her own retreat this year!

The community is full of heart-centered people, who love each other and are doing the real work, changing and healing their lives, so they can help others do the same. Little do they know that as soon as they begin sharing with and helping others, they will experience even deeper knowing and healing than what they facilitate.

Overwhelmed with gratitude to be doing what I love, and seeing the evidence of my magic egg finally being expressed in the world, I fell into child's pose and wept.

Thank you. Thank you. Thank you. Thank you for guiding me from my Magic Egg to my Butterfly Impact. How could it get better than this? And yet, somehow, I know it will…

> Overwhelmed with gratitude to be doing what I love, and seeing the evidence of my magic egg finally being expressed in the world, I fell into child's pose and wept.

Just Be You

My dear, sweet Aaron. My prayer for you is that you will have many moments like the ones I had that day on that yoga mat — being swept away in awe of the divine design of this Life, the part we are given to play in it, and the joyful gratitude of moving and flowing with the process of transforming and choosing impact.

My prayer is that you will always love and nurture your Magic Egg — always give the greater part of your time and energy to that divine part of you that is not only destined for great Joy and Impact, but contains everything you need to become and do.

…that you will always remember what a powerful mirror you are to everyone you meet, and that you will find your way of relaxing into that truth. Your light shines so bright, naturally and beautifully, that it reflects back to everyone else the areas they need to heal and love. Please try to remember that when they act crazy, or mean, or sad, it's usually about them, not you. It may not feel like it at first, but letting your Magic Egg shine actually gives the people around you permission to rediscover and heal theirs. Just don't dim it.

…that you will always pay attention when someone steps into your space and mirrors something back to you. We are all mirrors for each other, and people will cross your path to help you see, heal, and become more of who you already are. It may make you feel angry, sad, or crazy for a little while — a little upside-down — but it's good. And it's easier if you relax into it and give yourself the safe space to transform. Be careful with yourself and others. This upside-down thing can be scary.

No matter what, I pray that you always remember that JUST BEING YOU already completely transformed my life...

...that you will be the first to love yourself, even when you see something you don't like. I hope you will do the same thing for yourself that you did for me — allow yourself to just be you, to honor and feel and express your feelings, to reconnect with that part of you that has that answer, to stay committed to your own safety, and to just love yourself through the process.

...that you will always listen to that part of you that knows when you are ready and when you need more time. I have so enjoyed watching you develop the strength of your wings — your voice, your talents, and your compassion — and I know that you already know how to take your time and break through when you're ready.

...that you will always trust your own voice and stay connected to that still, small voice that is always there to tell you what is best for you and those around you. You know. You always have, and it will always be there for you.

...that you will always keep your eyes on your Impact — choosing who you are being in the world and doing what you are here to do. As you seek to share deep joy, abundance, love, and healing with others, you will experience even more of it yourself.

No matter what, I pray that you always remember that JUST BEING YOU already completely transformed my life...

...that you are loved and supported unconditionally...

...that you cannot mess this up...

Life has your back...

And so do I...

About

Amanda

As a Transformational Message Coach, Amanda Johnson helps aspiring or struggling speakers, authors, coaches… and now parents…change their lives and their world with powerful messaging.

After years of engaging, clarifying, and helping others develop powerful messages as a Student, a Teacher, and a Master Writing Coach, Amanda uncovered her own Message. The decision to take what she had learned with her son and share it with the world launched her on a journey of healing and transformation that quickly made her disconnected and depressed life completely unrecognizable.

Realizing how powerful a Message can be — not only for the audience, but for the Messenger — Amanda integrated everything she had learned from some of the world's most outstanding educators, powerful transformational coaches, and heart-centered business experts, and grew her business by 250% in just 18 months.

Today, she supports others in developing, branding, and monetizing their Message...and staying True to their Intention!

And now, with her original Message captured in *Upside-Down Mommy*, Amanda is determined to start a revolution with "The Butterfly Approach to Parenting" — an approach that invites the parent to carefully choose the messages they are speaking and modeling to their children...and to themselves.

An Important Invitation

from Amanda

True to Intention
What if Your Message IS the Answer?

FREE 30-Day Membership in the
Upside-Down Parent Cocoon-munity

What if you could raise your child with no limits?
What if you could live without yours?

It's possible, *and* it's a journey — a journey that is easier when you are surrounded by other parents who are doing the work, and by people who can help you move through it more quickly. If you've read this book, you know that *everything* in my life was a mess when this journey started for me — my health, my relationships, my finances... everything. It took years of working with several different coaches, healers, and experts to heal these areas and begin living, loving, and becoming with ease and joy.

But I Want to Make It Easier for You with...

- 🦋 **Monthly training/coaching calls** designed to give you the safe and sacred space where you can celebrate your successes and get the support you need to move through your breakdowns

- 🦋 **Monthly calls with supportive coaches with expertise** in healing relationships, finances, health, businesses, and so much more...

- 🦋 **MP3 Recordings** of *The Butterfly Approach to Parenting Retreatcamp* Training and Homework

- 🦋 **Private Upside-Down Parent Facebook Cocoon-munity**

If you're ready to **get started with ongoing training and support** on this journey of **healing and integrating *The Butterfly Approach to Parenting***, then this opportunity is for you. The True to Intention Community has designed a virtual parent coaching and training **Upside-Down Parent Cocoon-munity** that allows you to have instant access to the **support that you need, when you need it.**

If you would like to experience the support of this community and TRY IT **FREE for 30 days**, go directly to **www.UpsideDownParentCocoon.com** to get all of the details and sign up. In addition to the training and support, you will also receive MP3 recordings via email monthly, so you can download and listen to them anytime in your busy mommy (or daddy) life. Don't wait! **This type of support will help you change your relationship with your children and your life!**

If you desire more intensive training or support, please visit **www.UpsideDownMommy.com** to learn more about our *Upside-Down Mommy (and Daddy) Training and Coaching programs and LIVE transformational retreats.*

As our **special gift to you**, you will also receive an MP3 audio download *What's Your True Intention*...just for signing up!